Royal Academy of Arts

Year Book

Royal Academy of Arts

Year Book

ROYAL ACADEMY OF ARTS, LONDON 1981–82

published in association with

AIDAN ELLIS

The Royal Academy of Arts and the publisher, Aidan Ellis, would like to thank all those responsible for the exhibitions held during the year, without whom this publication would not be possible.

The Year Book is a record of events held at the Royal Academy during the year. Please refer to the individual exhibition catalogues for further information.

Other colour separations by:
Nensele Litho Ltd., Italy
The Meriden Gravure Company, U.S.A.
Giunti Barbèra, Italy
Meisenbach Riffarth & Co., Berlin (West)
TPS, London
Gavin Martin Ltd.

First published in Great Britain by Aidan Ellis Publishing Ltd.,
Cobb House, Nuffield, Henley-on-Thames, Oxon RG9 5RU

British Library Cataloguing in Publication Data
Royal Academy
    Royal Academy (Year Book) – 1981
    1. Art museums – Periodicals – England
    I. Title
    708.2'132'005   N9.A12/
ISBN 0 85628 108 5
Set in Monophoto Bembo and printed by Balding & Mansell, Wisbech.

Contents

Programme of Exhibitions 1980–81

Preface

In 1981, The Royal Academy welcomed to Burlington House over a million visitors. This Yearbook – the first of a planned series – is a record of what they came to see.

For some, it will be a record of past pleasures enriched, I hope, by the comments of our expert contributors. For many others, it will, perhaps, be a revelation: there can surely be no unsubsidised art institution in the world which could boast of a programme so varied in scope and distinguished in quality. Treasures from one of England's stateliest homes, authoritative retrospections of the work of celebrated English and Foreign artists, the famous Summer Exhibition held uninterruptedly for over 200 years and culminating in the most spectacular, ambitious and costly exhibition ever mounted at Burlington House – The Great Japan Exhibition.

Proud as we are of all this, we recognise none of it could have been achieved without the help of others . . . the owners and generous lenders of works of art, the sponsors who have come enthusiastically to our financial aid, the general public and, above all, our ever increasing Company of loyal Friends.

May I express our thanks to all of them and also our hope that as many as possible will enjoy this modest account of our joint endeavours past and yet to come.

HUGH CASSON

Post-Impressionism

Rediscovery is for the unknown or the forgotten. How is it possible for something so totally known, so obsessively remembered in the orisons of art buyers as the Post-Impressionists to be rediscovered? What painters are more famous, more sought-after, than Van Gogh or Gauguin? And yet, the Royal Academy's *Post-Impressionism* show in the winter of 1979–80 came with the force of a revelation.

It was not for the first time in British art history. Probably the most influential show this century, on the widest variety of artists and art-lovers, was *Manet and the Post-Impressionists* at the Grafton Galleries from November 1910 to February 1911. Forty years later Frank Dobson recalled the occasion for students at the Royal College of Art: "Post-Impressionism awakened me from my enchanted dream. The show at the Grafton Galleries was just an explosion – the demolition of all the art forms I had come to know. I was affronted, even hurt. But what a vista!" And he was by no means alone. The show (along with the arrival of Diaghilev's Ballets Russes shortly afterwards) was instrumental in flushing a whole generation – several generations, in fact – of British art with colour; in a recent show at the National Portrait Gallery one could see what a radical effect it had on even such an essentially conservative painter as William Strang, who suddenly forsook old-master chiaroscuro for a virtual pastiche of Gauguin.

And of course the influence was most powerfully felt within the orbit of the show's deviser, Roger Fry. The show itself was designed in virtual illustration of the thesis Fry had put forward the previous year to challenge the art establishment in his "Essay on Aesthetics", which concluded with the brisk announcement: "We may, then, dispense once and for all with the idea of likeness to Nature, of correctness or incorrectness as a test, and consider only whether the emotional elements in natural form are adequately discovered." Obedient to this view of painting and its functions, the show included 21 works each by Van Gogh and Cézanne, and no fewer than 41 by Gauguin, along with eight by Manet, proposed as the origin of everything worthwhile in contemporary French painting, which embraced for Fry's purposes Matisse (25 works), Vlaminck (11 works) and assorted Symbolists, Nabis and Fauves such as Redon, Denis and Derain.

According to Desmond MacCarthy, who wrote the catalogue introduction after Fry's notes, Fry considered calling the movement he had invented for the British public – Expressionism. (If he had, one wonders, what would have Expressionism have been called?) But finally he settled for "Post-Impressionism", which had the advantage of tying the painters gathered under this heading down to nothing more committing than a place in time, somewhere after the Impressionists. All the same, by its concentration on Gauguin and Van Gogh among the already dead, and Matisse among the living, the show did suggest some generalisations about the group. In particular, it seemed to identify them as expressive (if not expressionist) users of dazzling colour.

It is salutary to observe what even some of the most sympathetic commentators on the show thought of the newer painters included. C. J. Holmes, for example, who was on the exhibition committee and wrote a much-used book of notes on the show for visitors, found the essence of Post-Impressionism in "the greatest possible vibrancy and luminosity of colour, obtained by the juxtaposition of pure bright pigment in small separate touches," and "rigid simplification . . . in which the means of expression are reduced to line and colour, unbroken (or practically so) by shadows or by attempts at surface modelling". But then in the body of the book he comes up with some very surprising judgements indeed. For instance, of Picasso's *Nude Girl with Basket of Flowers*: "Pretty colour, clever planning, and an attractive model combine to make this one of the most obviously popular things in the gallery. Yet its charm is one of accomplishment, not of real power, and something academic (in the London use of the word) underlies its show of frankness. Mr Solomon J. Solomon in different surroundings might have painted thus." After which, it is not surprising to find him remarking: "If M. Picasso is best understood by a comparison with Mr Solomon, M. Maurice Denis is best understood if we think of him as a French Waterhouse!"

And yet Holmes was a model of understanding. Though the *Daily Express* noted that "Belgravia and Mayfair are flocking to the galleries, taking the colour cure for depression. The Post-Impressionists have become a cult," the critic of *The Nation* sounded a serious warning note: "If English art is not to be dragged in the mud, if we are to uphold the great traditions of the past . . . such exhibitions as this must cease, for disease and pestilence are apt to spread." Fortunately the warning went unheeded, and the Post-Impressionist disease spread like wildfire in the next few years – at any rate, as far as the admission of brilliant colour to British painting was concerned.

Much the same could be said of the Academy show's after-effects in 1980. If there was one thing which obviously and immediately distinguished the contents of the 212th Summer Exhibition from those of the 211th, it was the sudden flash and dazzle of colour on all sides. And the ripples continue. It does not seem too far-fetched, for instance, to guess that the violent colour of David Hockney's last group of large Los Angeles paintings, unveiled in the Academy's *New Spirit in Painting* show, may well have had something to do with the impact of the *Post-Impressionism* show a year previously. Certainly the impetus must have come from somewhere for Hockney to make such a striking departure from his previous practice.

As may be gathered, what modern artists seem to have picked up from the show was, as with the Grafton Galleries one, an approach to colour noticeably different from that which had thitherto been in vogue. And colour must have been the most immediate impression any visitor to the show received, since that was, in this show, far wider-ranging than the first, the principal thing linking an otherwise extraordinarily disparate group. For it could be said of the Post-Impressionists – and no doubt this was implicit in Fry's choice of a label – that a group so large and varied can hardly be regarded as a group at all, let alone something as coherent as a movement.

No doubt the first mistake in relation to the show would be even to look for that kind of coherence. Much better to take it on the same sort of terms as the Council of Europe shows which summon up a panorama of an age in all its diversity and contradictions. One movement Post-Impressionism certainly was not; not even anything as vague as a shift of taste in any one direction. But the Post-Impressionist period – say, from about 1885 to 1910 – does show an alarming number of shifts, in an alarming number of directions: movement follows movement, and style follows style, with bewildering rapidity, even within the work of individual painters, and sometimes, to make matters worse, they seem to be going in what should, according to all our theories, be the wrong direction. What are we to make of the "retreat" made by Toorop and Van de Velde in the early 1890s from the fully developed, magisterially confident Pointillist or Neo-Impressionist style of *The Shell Gatherer* or *Bathing-Huts on the Beach at Blankenberghe* to Toorop's mystical Symbolism and Van de Velde's curvilinear Art Nouveau furniture and decoration?

But then, if this puts us on our guard about any simple, all-inclusive formulation of the high road to modern art, it is all to the good. Evidently, from this show, the notion that Paris was the natural centre of the art world and what happened there, in natural, organic development (conveniently disregarding anything that did not fit in) from Impressionism to Pointillism to the very specific Post-Impressionism of the Pont Aven group, then through to the Nabis and thence, joining up again with late Cézanne, to Analytical Cubism and on, was the main stream of art, has to be radically re-thought. The way that the exhibition was organised began by setting up this traditional view for us in six rooms devoted to French art (with a rather puzzling eruption of British art 1880–1895 along the way), then carefully beginning to dismantle the arrangement it had so painstakingly assembled.

This it did by the simple expedient of starting to remind us that all sorts of things were going on in other European countries beside France. (The picture might have been diversified even further by the addition of Russia and – as was done in the Washington follow-up to the show – America.) The Neo-Impressionist work of Toorop and Van de Velde, shown alongside their French fellows, led naturally enough to a room of art from the Low Countries. But there things began perceptibly to fall apart. Not only did Toorop go off at a tangent, but how, according to Paris-centred orthodoxy, was one to account for the scribbly grotesques of Ensor, or the wispy symbols of Khnopff? And from there on things got stranger and stranger. Munch from Norway and Hodler from Switzerland and Kirchner from Germany (in his very early works) might well belong to that alternative Northern Romantic Tradition proposed by Robert Rosenblum, which manages also, on its wayward course, to rope in Van Gogh. But apart from that connection there seems to be no way that all these painters can comfortably be brought into the same frame.

The next room devoted to the French painters of the 1890s did, it is true, fulfil the chronological requirement: later than the Impressionists they certainly were, and no doubt such fashionable portraitists as Jacques-Emile Blanche and Giovanni Boldini (included here for his Parisian clientele in spite of his Italian birth) did learn something from the Impressionists, as, quite possibly, did Henri Martin with his classical idyll *Sérénité*, though its debt to Puvis de Chavannes is such that it too seems to belong to an alternative tradition, of rather literary painting in France, which might have continued along the same lines even if the Impressionists had never existed.

Funnily enough, the British painters of the Camden Town Group and the Bloomsbury Group seem to be the truest and most obvious adherents to Post-Impressionism in some strict sense of the term: quite likely because the 1910 show had such a deep and lasting effect on them, directly and through the teaching and example of Roger Fry. With the Italian room we were again off on a tangent, though a very interesting and in this country little-known one. Obviously painters like Segantini, Pellizza and early Balla were going in roughly the same direction as their French contemporaries, but in their own rather different fashion: a style akin to Pointillism dominated the work of many, but apparently much less scientifically defined, and using, on the whole, little strokes of colour to build up a restless, shimmering surface.

So, the ultimate effect of the show was, obviously, an *embarras de richesses*, confusing in its details yet oddly coherent as a whole – coherent, mainly because of that overriding flavour of a particular period which suffuses retrospectively all sorts of, in their day, wildly disparate things done, as their creators supposed, in the cause of completely opposing aesthetics. The big question mark hanging over the show was undoubtedly: was there ever such a thing as a single Post-Impressionist aesthetic, something to which all the artists concerned might be supposed more or less to subscribe to, something which, when applied as a yardstick in dubious cases, would enable us to separate the sheep from the goats? The answer to that has, I think, to be no. Holmes's formulation, arrived at in any case after the event, and by someone who was not in any way himself connected with the supposed movement, would, it is true, cover quite a number of the artists represented in the 1980 show, as it covered most, but not even then really all, of those shown in 1910. But still the bit about rigid simplification excludes as many as it includes, and finally we find ourselves left with just something vague about brilliance of colour.

Perhaps we do not need any more. Obviously all the artists who seem in the time since the R.A. show to have added a new brilliance to their palette did not: the general impression was liberation enough. However, to look in more detail at the show and its implications it is as well to get our bearings first. This is especially necessary in that, with such a complicated subject to cover and so many pictures somehow to organise (428 catalogued), it was inevitable that any arrangement would be in some way confusing. No doubt the arrangement hit upon by the show's organisers was as coherent as any: a compromise between national and chronological. But it had the twin disadvantage of perpetuating the Francocentric view of art history at this time (everything began in France, then fanned out over the rest of Europe) and of obscuring reasonably distinct and independent lines of development by putting unlikes which happened to coincide chronologically together rather than with earlier and later examples of their own kind.

This was particularly unfortunate in that the show proved to be about not something coherent which could be confidently labelled Post-Impressionism, but rather the world of art in which the Post-Impressionists proper (or as we would normally, if loosely, understand the term) appeared, functioned and were eventually absorbed. This was, to begin with, the world of the Impressionists, who, needless to say, were not all swept neatly from the scene in the early 1880s, and did not all noticeably deviate from their set courses when the first Post-Impressionists, which is to say Seurat and his Neo-Impressionist or Pointillist associates, made a sudden sensation in the last Impressionist show of 1886. True, we could see in this show the effect that they had on one of the major Impressionists, Pissarro, particularly in one of the finest of all his paintings, *L'Ile Lacroix, Rouen, Effect of Fog* (1888), but even he reverted afterwards to a more classic Impressionist style. And as for Cézanne or Monet or Renoir, the degree to which they were Impressionist in the first place (arguable in Cézanne's case) and to which they developed beyond Impressionism in later years are complicated enough without our trying to tie them in with Post-Impressionism. While anyone might well be mystified as to what Manet is doing there at all, unless he knew that Roger Fry had stated categorically that he should be.

But the Impressionists were not the only forerunners and independent contemporaries of the Post-Impressionists. At the time even in France there were other equally significant and influential movements, though they have tended until recently to be overlooked in a Hegelian desire to establish organic patterns of development in the arts, with one direct line and the rest negligible branch-lines and dead ends. For example, there was a whole school of rural Realists with a passionate belief in the physical necessity, and it seemed the moral excellence, of *plein-air* painting. Jules Bastien-Lepage effectively started the movement; unlike the Impressionists he stayed happily in the bosom of the Paris Salon up to his death, at the age of 36 in 1884. The one painting by him in the R.A. show, *Poor Fauvette* (1881), gives a clear idea of his style and approach, and his influence is very obvious on French painters such as Jean Charles Cazin with *Tobias and the Angel* (1880), English painters like Clausen (*The Stone Pickers*, 1886) and La Thangue (*Return of the Reapers*, 1886), and a whole school of Scottish painters, the so-called Kailyard School, whose work was fairly represented by James Guthrie's *A Hind's Daughter* (1883).

Now none of these paintings seems to have anything noticeable to do with Post-Impressionism in either of Holmes's usual senses, and would have made much more sense grouped together as a separate movement, parallel to Impressionism, which maybe contributed something to the Post-Impressionist ferment. Certainly Clausen and La Thangue went over in the 1890s to a Post-Impressionist brilliance of colour, but to add to the confusion these paintings were not represented, and indeed the whole decade of British art was excluded on the surely unwarrantable assertion that at that period "British artists deliberately eschewed foreign influences in favour of national traditions".

Then again, there was the Symbolist strain. Earlier, isolated French figures such as Gustave Moreau and Puvis de Chavannes were included with little explanation as to their relevance or lack of it (as, indeed, was the still more isolated painter Adolphe Monticelli, whose improvisatory brush-strokes and sometimes garish colour were an important influence on Van Gogh and a number of Scots). Whereupon there followed quite mysteriously later French Symbolists like Redon, Germans of a more academic cast like Ludwig Von Hofmann and Franz Von Stuck, both with elaborate symbolic compositions, and the sinuous Art Nouveau work of the Dutch Johannes Thorn Prikker and Jan Toorop in his 1890s post-Neo-Impressionist phase, though not, oddly enough, that of Xavier Mellery, best known for his hefty symbolic pieces but here represented only by *After Evening Prayers* of c.1890, a soberly coloured realistic interior with nuns. Why, one might wonder, go so far with the Symbolists, or if so far, why not further?

Nor were the unabashed academic painters of the period wholly neglected. Of course, one could make a case for some influence from the Impressionists on even the most stuffy, Establishment figures: the situation in French art in the 1880s was rather similar to that of English drama when Bernard Shaw commented that "A modern manager need not produce *The Wild Duck*, but he must be very careful not to produce a play which will seem insipid and old-fashioned to playgoers who have seen *The Wild Duck*, even though they may have hissed it". Academic painters, or *artistes pompiers*, did not have to become Impressionists, but they could not afford to ignore altogether the lessons of the Impressionists. Which is no doubt the explanation of the brilliantly rendered pearly morning light in Gaston La Touche's *Pardon in Brittany* (1896), though La Touche was the darling of the Salon and the official artist *par excellence* of the 1890s. Similarly one can understand, if not quite explain away, the presence of the fashionable Besnard ("Besnard is flying with our wings," said Dégas) or the saucy nymphs of Paul Chabas, enjoying *Happy Frolics* in the shallows (1899), though Albert Maignan's faintly absurd *The Passage of Fortune* (an allegorical lady whisks alarmingly past soberly clad bystanders on the steps of the Stock Exchange) did seem to be pushing a point rather further than it could reasonably be taken.

And those are all confusions which start in France, even if they become worse confounded elsewhere. The show, which began in fairly leisurely fashion with a generous selection of French artists -- indeed, if anything over-inclusive – suddenly speeded up disturbingly to rush through the rest, with insufficient opportunity to work out whether Germany, say, or Italy, had anything which could be assessed as an independent tradition, a specific local flavour at least, in painting which could be accounted chronologically Post-Impressionist. Against all odds, something distinctive did emerge from Italy: not only the particular technical approaches of Italian Divisionism, but a widespread interest in social and even political themes for painting – something which, to judge from the evidence available, was almost totally lacking in French painting of the time (Luce's *The Iron Foundry* of 1899 is a rare exception in the form of an unmistakably industrial scene). It is not for nothing that the single painting in the Academy show which seems to have left an indelible impression on most visitors (and not only because of its size), Pellizza's *The Fourth Estate* (1901), a statement of solidarity with the advancing proletariat, also featured with no less appropriateness as the cover illustration for the catalogue of the immediately preceding Milan exhibition *Arte e Socialità in Italia dal realismo al Simbolismo, 1865–1915*.

On the other hand, there was no knowing at the Academy whether painters like the Norwegian Munch or the Swiss Hodler were isolated phenomena, working out their own artistic salvations largely in isolation (in fact, that is a fair enough description of their very different careers). Or how a mysterious figure like Liebermann fitted into European art: actually, a vast recent Berlin retrospective suggests that he fitted in obligingly just about everywhere except with Post-Impressionism. Or, despite the presence of early works by Heckel, Kirchner and others, quite what in previous German art Die Brücke sprang from, and whether it was really a close German equivalent of the Fauve group in Paris. And if the picture the show presented of the Camden Town group, the Bloomsbury Group and other elements of the London art scene in the 1900s seemed more coherent,

Georges Seurat   *Le Crotoy, Looking Upstream*   *Post-Impressionism*

Louis Hayet   *River Landscape*   *Post-Impressionism*

Edouard Vuillard   *The Stevedores*   *Post-Impressionism*

Maurice Denis   *Procession under the Trees*   *Post-Impressionism*

Louis Anquetin   *Street – Five o'clock in the Evening*   *Post-Impressionism*

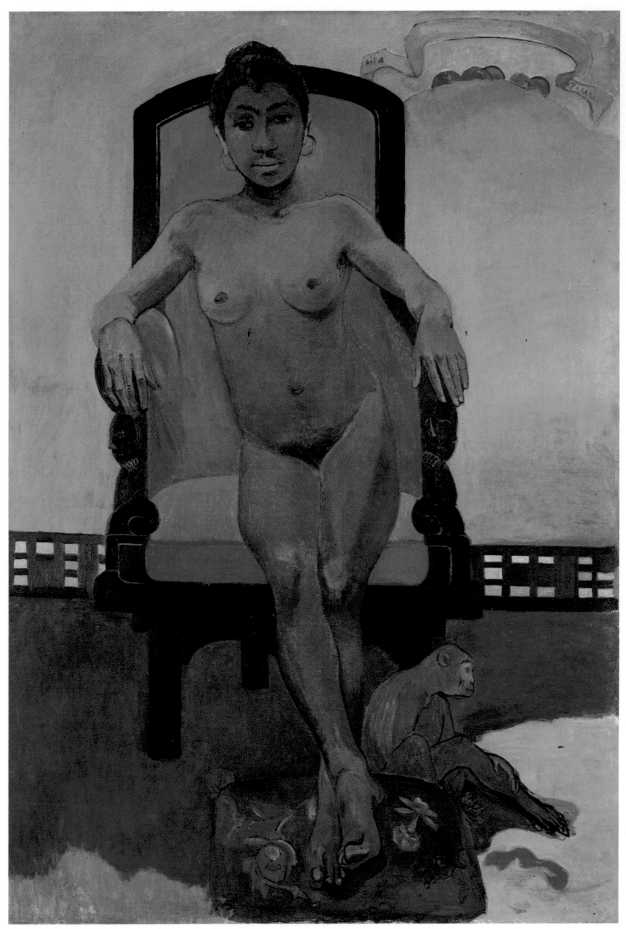

Paul Gauguin   *Annah the Javanese*   *Post-Impressionism*

Paul Cézanne *Undergrowth*

Vincent Van Gogh   *The Olive Pickers*   *Post-Impressionism*

Vincent Van Gogh   *Poppy Field*   *Post-Impressionism*

Théo Van Rysselberghe *Family in Orchard*   *Post-Impressionism*

Guiseppe Pellizza da Volpedo *Washing in the Sun*   *Post-Impressionism*

Jules Bastien-Lepage *Poor Fauvette*

Walter Richard Sickert   *L'hôtel Royal, Dieppe*   *Post Impressionism*

Henri Edmond Cross   *La Pointe de la Galère*   *Post-Impressionism*

André Derain *Fishermen at Collioure*   *Post-Impressionism*

Philip Wilson Steer *Boulogne Sands*   *Post-Impressionism*

Jan Toorop   *The Shell Gatherer*   *Post-Impressionism*

Giovanni Segantini   *Rest in the Shade*   *Post-Impressionism*

Odilon Redon   *The Red Sphinx*

Albert Dubois-Pillet
Saint Michel d'Aiguilhe in the Snow

Giacomo Balla   *The Worker's Day*

Paul Signac   *Portrait of M. Félix Fénéon in 1890*

Cuno Amiet
Reclining Breton Girl with Orange

Edvard Munch   *Ashes*

Maximilien Luce   *The Iron Foundry*

Louis Anquetin   *Gust of Wind: Bridge over the Seine*

Spencer Gore
Gauguins and Connoisseurs at the Stafford Gallery

Giovanni Segantini   *The Representation of Spring*

Camille Pissaro   *Ile Lacroix, Rouen, Effect of Fog*

Roger Fry   *Blythborough, The Estuary*

Emile Bernard   *Breton Women at a Pardon*

that was quite possibly because we know enough ourselves to fill in the details. (Though credit must be given to the show for unearthing Roger Fry's only really advanced, Post-Impressionist painting, *Blythborough, the Estuary* of 1892/3, which he never dared exhibit at the time and has remained almost unknown ever since.)

But one could go on carping for ever, and all the complaints would boil down to one: that the subject was so vast and, after all, surprisingly undefined that even a show twice the size could not have done complete justice to it and answered all the questions. As it was, exhausted visitors were liable to complain that there was altogether too much, certainly to be adequately taken in at one go. I never feel much sympathy with that point of view: I like to have as much as possible thrown at me, and make my own selection of parts deserving (or commanding) particular attention, and any other view seems to me like announcing, faced with *War and Peace*, that you never, on principle, read books more than 120 pages long. Some shows can afford to be selective and intimate: this could not. And the fact remains that, for all the possible excesses and confusions, the show did have an enormous impact on all who saw it. Perhaps not always for the "right" reasons. But then an impact is an impact: when it genuinely occurs it is not to be argued with.

One of the "wrong" reasons that many people have noted was that the admittedly great painters did not necessarily come off any better than, or even quite so well as, painters nobody would coolly qualify as anything but minor. To an extent, that is inevitable in a show of this nature. Even if the works of great painters selected are themselves great – which was maybe not possible with, for example, the biggest-ever show of Toulouse-Lautrec on at the same time in Chicago – they inevitably lack the element of surprise. We *expect* Gauguins and Van Goghs to be wonderful, and therefore merely recognise the wonder when we see it. We do not expect to be excited by a Gaston La Touche – we have quite possibly hardly heard of him – and therefore may well be disproportionately bowled over. All the same, while hardly urging us to wholesome demotion (even if the Van Goghs were a rather lack-lustre bunch), the show did encourage us to up several lesser-known painters a few notches, and note down several more for further exploration.

In the first category, for me, would come Louis Anquetin: his *Girl Reading a Newspaper* from the Tate Gallery is of course familiar, but his *Street – Five O'Clock in the Evening* (1887), with its bold colouring and at the same time amazingly precise evocation of a particular time of day at a particular season of the year, is a stunning painting in its own right, as well as being well ahead of its time. Even more astonishing in its own way is *Gust of Wind: Bridge Over the Seine* (1889), in which the essentially modern subject of fashionably dressed women clinging to their hats, and horses, their manes blown forward by the wind, in the foreground, is treated with the immediacy of an action-photograph and at the same time the delicately mannered patterning of a Japanese print. Disappointingly, the catalogue informs us that after various stylistic excursions, Anquetin "eventually settled on a Baroque style of monumental painting, indebted primarily to Rubens". So maybe he should not be upgraded too far, on the strength of a few paintings from a passing phase. All the same, the two unfamiliar paintings remain astonishing *tours de force*, worth, if necessary, going to Hartford, Connecticut or Bremen (respectively) to see.

A lot of painters shown come into the second category. It would be good, I am sure, to know more of Georges Lacombe, whose *Blue Seascape – Effect of Waves* (c. 1891) meets (quite fortuitously, no doubt) one of the best Gauguins in the show, *The Beach at Le Pouldu* (1889), on its own ground and suffers not a whit by the comparison. Or again, there is Albert Dubois-Pillet, a professional soldier throughout his adult life who died young (at 44 in 1890), one of whose two paintings in the show, *Saint Michel d'Aiguilhe in the Snow*, done just before his death, is one of the most vivid of all the Pointillist paintings. (In fact, I might note parenthetically, the room devoted to the Pointillists was, along with the room devoted to painters in Brittany associated with Pont Aven, the most exciting to me, making me think that I would now very much like to see these two specialised areas explored in shows of their own, which could go into them in much greater depth.)

Prospecting among less familiar artists could profitably go much further afield. If *Post-Impressionism* did not quite succeed in making obvious sense of all the ramifications of the period in all possible countries, and clearly threw up its hands at the prospect of having to add a section on a lot of, in Europe, totally unfamiliar Americans (J. Carter Brown tells us, in his introduction to the catalogue of the Washington version, where this omission was handsomely rectified, that it was originally the intention to include Americans in London, until sheer pressure of space forced them out), at least it must be acknowledged that much Western European art which had never previously been seen in this country made its appearance here for the first time and, in the context of such an event, made a powerful impression. One need only cite the effect this has had on the art market in London, leading on directly as it did to ambitious shows like *Fin de Siècle* and

Dreamers and Academics at the Louise Whitford Gallery, a notable extension of Roy Miles's interests from Victorian to Post-Impressionist, and many a flurry in the salerooms.

Ironically, the artists who seem to have attracted most attention were almost all non-French, and as a rule those in the show who could with least certainty be classed as Post-Impressionists at all. In all probability this is because turn-of-the-century Italian or Austrian art remains, even in its own country, a relatively uncharted area of collecting and scholarship. For many artists from such sources, the hefty catalogue constitutes a valuable dispenser of information and director towards further research: quite a new function of exhibition catalogues in Britain, though already familiar in Europe and the United States.

But finally one keeps coming back to the show as a memorable feast for the eye and the mind: in that order. It may be a partial explanation of the paucity of social comment or even clear-eyed study of contemporary life in Post-Impressionist painting, especially French, that this was above all painting about painting. Whether they knew the formulation or not, almost all the painters of the period paid some sort of obedience to the twenty-year-old Maurice Denis's observation in his *Définition du néo-traditionnisme*: "Remember that a painting, before it is a warhorse, a female nude or some little genre scene, is primarily a flat surface covered with colours arranged in a certain order." Whether the order was arranged in dots or dashes or areas of unmodelled colour with firm outlines, the concern was first and foremost with achieving (to use a term which nowadays has a derogatory ring to it) a satisfying decorative surface; what that surface told you, or allowed you to divine, about external reality, the world of dreams, or what might lie in between, was of varying importance from artist to artist, but always secondary. Even with an exceptional case, like Pellizza's *The Fourth Estate*, the effect is created not by means of literal reportage, but through a species of monumental abstraction, achieved – but of course – by the precise manner in which paint is applied to canvas.

As for what the eye took in before the mind had a chance to work on it, the predominant impression remains: colour, colour and yet more colour. Even when the attitude of the painters to their work was towards the ascetic side of aesthetic, as with the mystical Nabis grouped round Denis in Brittany, there is nothing self-denying about their use of colour: if God could be worshipped in the splendour of colour in medieval art, they saw no reason why that should be any the less so in their own day, and they determinedly rejected pallid good taste. In any case, a remote, hieratic quality, a sense of bejewelled richness, had a particular appeal to the Decadent sensibility, which crops up all over the art of the 1890s as an important, though not for long intellectually respectable, element. And beyond that there were many painters who, simple sybarites, just revelled in brilliant colour for its own sake, with no need of intellectual formulations to do with Charles Henri's theories on the physical mechanism of sight, let alone any of the Nabis' or the Salon de la Croix Rouge's transcendental and occult formulations.

Above all, *Post-Impressionism* was a happy show, warming in the raw London winter. For all the dark undertones present in the works of the Post-Impressionists, shadowing somewhat the Impressionists' Garden of Eden, they still convey a feeling of "Bliss was it in that dawn to be alive". The Impressionists had opened the windows, and light came flooding in. The Post-Impressionists went a few steps further, rejoicing in their new-found freedom: freedom to paint what they saw the way they felt it; freedom to revise and rearrange the shapes of reality if they chose, or look away from reality altogether. The delight of the Post-Impressionist era was its sheer lack of structure, the cheery refusal of its leading figures to do any one thing, go any one way, group themselves willy-nilly into a neat, coherent movement for the benefit of critics and art historians. In the galleries of the Royal Academy during the *Post-Impressionism* show, the sense of liberation was palpable on all sides. And liberation liberates. Some effects of the show have already been seen on the art of our own day. But, like as not, the best is yet to come.

JOHN RUSSELL TAYLOR

Stanley Spencer R.A.

Sacred to the Memory of
Sir Isaac Pocock Knight
Late of this parish
Who was suddenly called from this world to a better state
Whilst on the Thames, near his own house

In 1810, the year he became Professor of Sculpture at the Royal Academy, John Flaxman made a fine Neoclassical relief for the Pocock memorial in Cookham church. A ministering angel, garments awhirl, tends Sir Isaac while the boatman punts frantically for the shore.

The tone of the inscription and the image of the slumped figure clutching at his heart, the strangeness of the incident, topical yet timeless, local yet universalised in marble, the crisp outlines, the dramatic gestures, are uncannily Spencerian. Young Stan must have sat beside Cookham's Flaxman often enough and looked at it during sermons, enjoying the elegant flurry. It was from this, perhaps, that he derived the idea of the Thames as the river Styx. In *The Resurrection, Cookham* he put Bond's steam launch at the top left hand corner of the composition, behind the church, ferrying people from this world to the next. Sir Isaac, overcome with what was clearly intended to be interpreted as both death agony and the onset of eternal bliss, is the prototype of innumerable Cookhamites in Spencer's paintings. They lounge on the riverbank, sprawl in blazers on the grass during the unveiling of Cookham War Memorial. They plead for favours from bulky women, suffer temptation after temptation, awaken in the churchyard, rubbing their eyes and stretching themselves ready to face the Last Day.

At the very end of his life Stanley Spencer contemplated painting a Last Judgement, for Cookham church. He would have shown the Apostles sitting in committee, like members of the parish council, deciding the fate of the 12 tribes of

Israel. Once again the people of Cookham would have served as models, bit-players in the village pageant, herded together, backbiting to the last, rolling their eyes in lust or alarm, crying "Hosannah!" or simply gawping. It was always the same. Biblical events came to pass and were recorded with plentiful, Parish Magazine detail. *The Last Supper* took place in the Malt House in School Lane, *The Baptism*, as a Sunday School outing, at Odney Pool, *The Visitation* and *The Betrayal* at the bottom of the garden of Fernlea, the artist's birthplace. Christ – a strictly Nonconformist sort of Christ – carried the Cross along Cookham High Street, past Fernlea to the place of execution.

The High Street, with the stark white cross of the War Memorial at one end and the ancient Tarrystone at the other, was the scene of many untoward occurrences. *The Crucifixion* took place there, coinciding with extensive roadworks. Stanley's father, old William Spencer (Prof Wm Spencer as he styled himself) appeared from time to time outside Fernlea in nightgown and slippers, a patriarch come to berate. He told Stanley about Sarah Tubb, who used to sink to her knees and pray in the street, believing that the end of the world was at hand. In his painting *Sarah Tubb and the Heavenly Visitors*, Spencer showed her being reassured by angels, gathered on the pavement and pointing out to her, with picture postcards of the church, the river and Odney Pool for reference, that she had no need to fear: Heaven was Cookham, after all.

Like Sir Isaac, like Sarah Tubb, Stanley Spencer became a legendary Cookham figure. The image of the little man pushing his pramful of painting paraphernalia from his house to a promising spot, the gossip about his matrimonial affairs, his grubbiness, his manic energy, made him seem the most pronounced character in the village and, indeed, the most colourful artistic personality in England. And since it was he who appeared more than anyone else in his own paintings, scurrying round, making protestations of love, cleaning, expressing thanks, rapt, amazed, or staring out at himself, the mirror image, inevitably Spencer turns out to be the leading Cookhamite. "Cookham", as he was nicknamed by his fellow students at the Slade on account of his identification with the place, pictured Cookham as his Paradise, his Jerusalem. In 1958 he held an exhibition in the church in aid of the Restoration Fund. He was on hand much of the time to discuss or rather explain his works: *The Last Supper* with its assertive brickwork and the bare feet of the disciples hobnobbing down the middle of the picture, *The Odney Baptism* and the unfinished *Christ Preaching at Cookham Regatta*. Since his death the Wesleyan Chapel, which he used to attend with his mother, has been converted into the Spencer Gallery where *Christ Preaching* overshadows the rest, mainly because of its size and ghostly quality. Sections of the top and centre are filled with plump, craning figures. The remainder is just pencilled outlines and bare canvas. The famous capsized pram is parked alongside, dusty now, like a leftover from the last jumble sale.

That then is Stanley Spencer of Cookham, the artist born and reared a villager who remained one all his days, a "peasant artist" according to Herbert Read. This is a beguiling verdict. Like L. S. Lowry, Spencer is accorded special outsider status, seen as one who had to struggle for recognition well away from the fleshpot art establishments.

But this, of course, is a sentimental distortion of the truth about Spencer and his art. "Cookham" was indeed secure in his roots and bound up in his beginnings, certain of his local connections and standing. Cookham was the scene of many of his most vivid memories. He referred all his experiences, all he came across, back to Cookham as the one locality he really knew. That, however, did not mean he was a blinkered rustic. Spencer of Cookham was also Spencer of the Slade (Gold Medallist), Spencer of Macedonia (Private Spencer no. 100066/68th Field Ambulance), Burghclere Spencer, Hampstead Spencer and, eventually, Sir Stanley Spencer C.B.E., R.A.

The Royal Academy Stanley Spencer exhibition brought out the full range of his art but also, inevitably, the chatterbox continuity, the constant drumming of heels and lingering over heart-on-sleeve effects. It made the dominant themes more apparent than ever, the range of motifs changing remarkably little over 40 years, that "special brew of thoughts," he once said "when all the Stanleys, this me and that me, can come out like children coming out of school". From first to last, Spencer not only expressed a kind of Neo-Biblical zest for narrative and exhortation, but also a delight in pattern. This served him as the means of blending his designs, drawing crowds together and leading the eye over masses of rump and greenery. He was the would-be Mantegna, the Crivelli, of Georgian painting; he loved unison and procession. Never a dull moment; always something for the spectator to puzzle out or enjoy as a surprise interpretation.

Spencer's ambitions went in cycles. Early on he learnt from the Old Masters, notably those of the Italian Renaissance, by studying their effects from postcard reproductions, squaring up to them and paying homage. Richard Carline tells of the time Spencer dreamt he was out walking on Cookham Moor. "He met Signorelli standing like his figure of *Anti-Christ* in Orvieto Cathedral. Signorelli greeted him with a smile, saying 'Good evening, Spencer; I liked your picture in the New English'." Cookham became a substitute Florence, Siena or Assisi. Spencer posed his Cousin Jack behind the hedge in *Joachim among the Shepherds*, used Dot Wooster, the butcher's daughter, as Elizabeth in *The Visitation*, drew on themes from Piero della Francesca, Ghiberti and Giotto. It was a matter of converting Cookham into a *quattrocento* location, merging what he loved with what he admired, thereby achieving the semblance of an archaic-everywhere.

The awkwardness of much of his student work is part of its charm. There's an intensity and a simplicity, a feeling of awakening and discovery which he later thought he lost during the war. Those he painted were people he had grown up with, acting out Bible stories to his instructions. He had confidence and security. Then came the war, a period as an orderly at Beaufort Hospital and afterwards a posting overseas: experiences which obviously had a crucial impact. He complained about his comrades: "They do not like Dickens and have never heard of Meredith and Hardy. Their knowledge of art extends no further than the Picture Palace ... If I can enter these men's little interests and hopes, why can't they enter into mine? I read the Testament nearly all day, and because I do so, they presume I must be one of those priggish 'holy' sort, whereas in many things I have paganistic sentiments . . ."

Spencer was the odd man out, accused once, he indignantly complained, of being cowardly. He simultaneously emphasised his cultural superiority, his pluck and zeal, and at the same time betrayed a longing to be treated as one of the chaps. Significantly, in this letter of 1918 Spencer was at pains to emphasise both his reading (Spencer the bookworm) and his dissent ("paganistic sentiments"). He was well set to become the Cookham Wonder.

He returned home in 1918, took up his painting where he had left off (*Swan Upping*, set in Turk's Boatyard had to be finished) and set about aligning his Macedonian experience with what had gone before. The transition was trying. He had to attempt a more refined and monumental style while retaining the directness of his formative period. This was where the self-conscious Spencerian image began to get in the way of the work. The non-stop litany of Spencer predilections, the insistence, the delving for exact memories meticulously detailed, no grave unopened, no whim ignored, started up. Around 1920 he came to a virtual parting of the ways. He posed himself a choice of treatments: either the uncluttered, flattened Christ-in-a-nightgown manner or progressive intricacy. Instead of deciding right away he alternated.

The *Burghclere Chapel* paintings, his only major project to be carried through to completion (thanks to the Behrends who commissioned it and provided the building) were the centrepiece of the Academy exhibition and, it is now clear, of his life's work. For there, faced with the task of covering three walls with a coherent pictorial scheme, adding predellas and thereby creating a testament with footnotes, he succeeded in identifying with his fellow-soldiers. For once he wasn't the village oddity but the indispensable professional, the recording angel.

Where in Renaissance frescoes the lives of the saints or the doings of princes would have been played out, at Burghclere the private soldier is exalted. Troops dig themselves in, bivouac, play housey-housey. They suffer injuries, enter the field hospital. They die and resurrect, surfacing dazedly somewhere near Kalinova on the Serbian border, casting aside barbed wire coil, stacking their crosses. In the paintings brought to Burlington House for the exhibition from Burghclere, Spencer is much in evidence, as an eager hospital orderly scrubbing floors ("I used to enjoy it rather"), rummaging the laundry, spreading thick slices of bread for the patients' tea. Out on the Macedonian Front he wanders through an encampment bayonetting torn pages of the "Balkan News", stuffing them into a sack. Fray Bentos tins, makeshift camouflage with ferns stuck into puttees, clanking tea urns, stray dogs, tortoises, pin-ups are the specifics that give these murals their extraordinary clarity; vision spiced with total recall.

These are war paintings without gunfire or heroics. Death means being fast asleep, dreaming of home. The telling details (mosquitoes seething in the roof of a bell tent, men floundering in the folds of the netting), the sharp eye for posture and gesture (washroom routines, sleeping habits), for the way the sun shines through gorse blossom and for the suede smoothness and pinkness of a mule pelt, were to remain Spencer's key characteristic.

However flaccid much of his later work proved to be, with the ideas running away and bubbling out of control, there was always the likelihood of some fine, pointed observation. For example, when he went to Port Glasgow in 1940 to draw and paint war work in the shipyards, it wasn't just the purposeful activity that fascinated him, the riveting, caulking, plumbing, joinery, rigging, but the curious domesticity, the cells and havens within the whale's belly of keel and girders.

The foreman, with his hands on his hips, dishing out orders like a paterfamilias in front of the sitting-room fire, the women looking on, the welders scorching their way across the vast steel plates as though scrambling over the eiderdown on the grown-ups' bed: Spencer was beside himself with delight. It was a sort of home from home. And, up on the hill, lay Port Glasgow cemetery; not so pretty as Cookham churchyard, certainly, but in its way more appropriate to his purpose. The gravestones, the tarmac pathways, the slopes leading down to the rooftops of the town and the Clyde beyond, the neat railings round each plot, the marble slabs inscribed like identity cards, were what attracted Spencer.

"I had the feeling that each grave forms a part of the person's home just as their front gardens do, so that a row of graves and a row of cottage gardens have much the same meaning for me. Also although the people are adult or any age, I think of them in cribs or prams or mangers."

So they wake up, dance, smile, hold hands and embrace. In Port Glasgow Spencer found collective activity such as he hadn't experienced since his army days. He darted round spotting key metaphors and reminders of old times. The shipbuilders were Cookham villagers and the Royal Berkshires redeployed. The themes circled and intertwined. One Resurrection after another, Cookham, Macedonia, Port Glasgow. Everyday events fitted into the perennial pattern of things, brought to that reassuring and everlasting state of happily-ever-after.

"Nothing is so tremendous as happiness which results from perfect truth," he wrote. Truth, to Spencer, meant the "happy hunting grounds" of his surroundings transfigured by his all-embracing imagination. He thought of getting someone to build a "Church House" for him, which he could flood with images, every wall covered with scenes of total reconciliation. Past and present would combine there. His first wife, Hilda, would be singled out for celebration, but there would be room too for his other wife, Patricia Preece, for Elsie the maid, for Sarah Tubb, St. Francis, Christ, blacks, collies, Friesians, Dalmatians, dandelions, old men, dustmen. The whole, marvellous creation would be a hymn to Love, a riot of joy.

Nothing came of it, apart from pencil drawings and a quantity of paintings, mostly of modest, saleable size, such as *Sarah Tubb and the Heavenly Visitors* and *The Dustman or The Lovers* and a series *The Beatitudes of Love* involving himself, among others, courting, ogling, pressing up against, falling head over heels in love with the objects of his affection. Running through the whole was Spencer's fervent, frenetic monotone, expressed in terms of painting, as insistent patterning. Herringbone tweeds, floral cottons, bulging forms covered in checks and polka dots, were herded on to Cookham Moor to worship a buxom Venus, open hat boxes and try on new clothes. He beavered away, intent on nothing but pressing home his violent desires and his corresponding fears, no matter if the characters were dummies, the ideas repetitive, the treatment wholesale. The pale, doughy people promenading, nattering, pairing off, flaunting their Sunday best, had idiosyncracies galore. They were also typical. But, increasingly, Spencer's acute observation became overlaid with hum-drum harmonies of form and colouration.

If Cookham was the making of Stanley Spencer it was also his salvation. Nowhere else offered the same concentration of associations and suggestive incident. His rare trips abroad, to Yugoslavia in 1922, to Switzerland in 1936 and to China in 1954 didn't even have the effect of disorientating him. He tried painting his experiences as a tourist. *Souvenir of Switzerland* was an attempted encapsulation of "Swiss feeling" with the people dressed in colourful local costume and an Alpine village treated almost in poster terms: the land of the cuckoo clock. In China he painted the Ming Tombs, in a snapshot style. At the Peking Art Academy he talked to the students for some hours with great enthusiasm, they remember, without bothering to wait for his words to be translated. Wherever he went he took his pet certainties with him, and the art that came out of these expeditions (also those to St. Ives, Southwold and Snowdonia) was plain travelogue.

But then for much of his life, the work that sold, that his dealer Dudley Tooth encouraged him to produce in order to make a living and buy himself time, was landscape. He used to complain that this was a waste of energy, a sideline in pot-boilers. It involved doing away with figures, concentrating on setting alone. So instead of straining and rhapsodising in votive or impassioned vein, Spencer settled down in front of the Tarrystone, the Jubilee tree near the War Memorial. He painted the Michaelmas daisies in Bellrope Meadow, the shingle at Southwold, the crazy paving behind Turk's Boatyard, greenhouses, a helter-skelter in the Vale of Health, Port Glasgow Cemetery. "My landscape painting has enabled me to keep my bearings," he admitted. "It has been my contact with the world, my soundings taken, my plumb line dropped." Landscape anchored him, rooted him to the spot, made him pause and consider instead of rambling on. Depopulated, Spencer's landscapes have an abandoned look. Everyone's at church or gone off to the wars. The punts lie at their moorings. A may tree foams with blossom whiter, even more bubbly than the soap suds he studied with such care in his Hampstead studio in preparation for the floorscrubbing scene in the Burghclere murals. The front gardens are deserted, the graves are unattended. Across a Dorset hillside barrack huts are lined up, their roofs glinting in the sunshine. A scarecrow extends its arms over a row of sweet peas, as though in benediction. "I liked the feeling of it always being there," he wrote. The scarecrow served as the model for a Crucifixion.

Every pebble, every blade of grass, every dollop of may blossom, every cabbage stalk and wisteria bloom was shown to deserve attention. The best of Spencer's straight, seemingly unimaginative paintings are an essential counter-balance to the more pneumatic fanciful set-pieces. The details stare back at you. Normality looks ominous. In the prosaic landscapes he made discoveries.

Then there was the flesh. "I want to be able to paint a nude from life and do it as I do a portrait. I mean not so quickly but taking my time." Between 1935 and 1937 Spencer painted Patricia Preece several times, her body awkwardly bent to fit the canvas, her attention diverted. In the most disconcerting of these, Spencer crouches over her in front of the Valor stove. Her thighs, her sagging breasts, are living meat. A leg of mutton and a lamb chop placed alongside emphasise the point. Spencer eyes her through his round specs, contemplating her, pondering the mystery of "male, female and animal flesh". He added "There is none of my usual imagination in this thing: it is direct from nature and my imagination never works faced with objects or landscape . . ."

Yet here Spencer brought himself face to face with the inescapable. The facts of his life lay exposed: the surge of desire, the waning to indifference even disgust; the state of intimacy; bared bodies but, however much he talked, right through the night, ultimate separateness. The nude paintings imply despair, not simply because Spencer's relationship with Patricia Preece was, one way and another, disastrous, but because they are inanimate and glum. In *Self Portrait with Patricia* she is on a bed, her eyes downcast. He looks sideways, like a heraldic eaglet, the folds of his neck muscles, the curves of her breasts and thighs, the rumpled sheets, the daisy motifs bursting on the wallpaper behind, as clear-cut, as rhythmic as the lines of a neoclassical bas-relief. This is death in life.

Sir Isaac Pocock, ferried across the river, expiring in the arms of his angel, reappears in the withdrawn, seemingly resentful person of Patricia Preece, adrift in the bed. Stanley, combining the roles of boatman and Heavenly Visitor, is preoccupied with his dreams of Love and Resurrection, that Better State where life is redeemed through art.

WILLIAM FEAVER

The Bathing Pool, Dogs

Stanley Spencer, R.A.

Swan Upping at Cookham   *Stanley Spencer, R.A.*

The Resurrection, Cookham

Stanley Spencer, R.A.

The Vale of Health, Hampstead   *Stanley Spencer, R.A.*

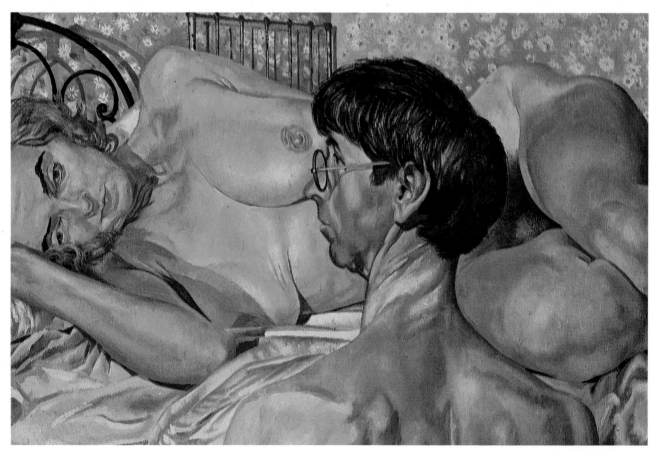

Self-Portrait with Patricia Preece   *Stanley Spencer, R.A.*

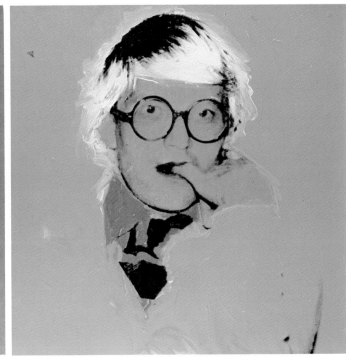

Andy Warhol   *Portrait of David Hockney*

Malcolm Morley *The Lonely Ranger Lost in the Jungle of Erotic Desires*

R. B. Kitaj   *The Jewish School (Drawing a Golem)*

A New Spirit in Painting

Julian Schnabel   *St. Francis in Ecstacy*

Frank Auerbach *Julia Asleep* (detail)

A New Spirit in Painting

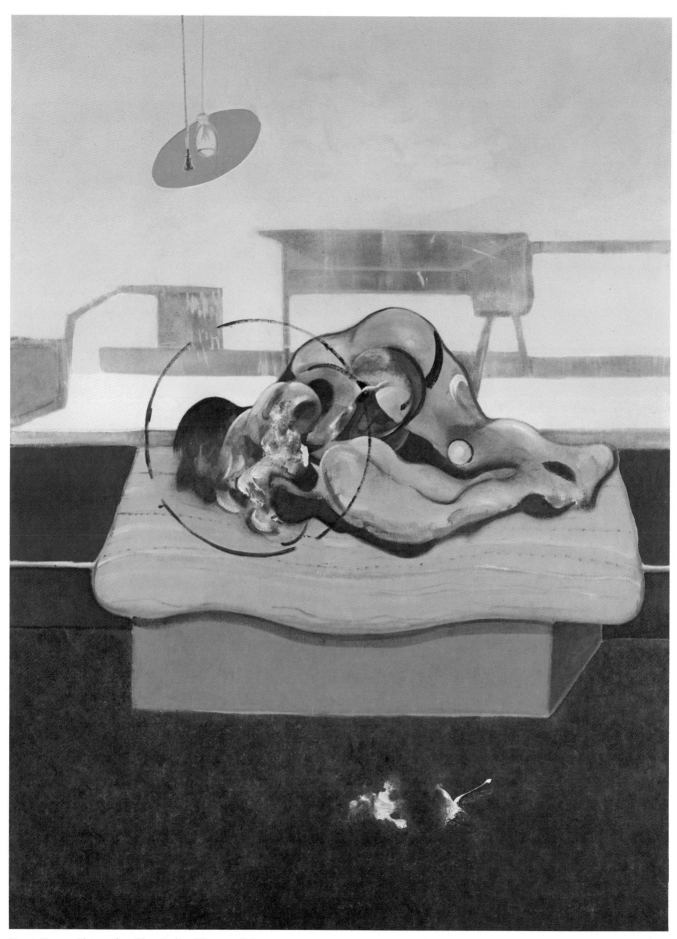

Francis Bacon   *Plate one from Three Studies of Figures on Beds*

A New Spirit in Painting

Balthus *Le Chat au Miroir*

Howard Hodgkin   *Dinner at Smith Square*

A New Spirit in Painting

A New Spirit in Painting, the show that only came about because an unexpected opening occurred in the Royal Academy's schedule, has turned out to be the most talked about show of the year. In fact, just about the only aspect of it which everyone in the art world agreed on was just how controversial it was.

International survey shows of current painting are rare, but not unique. The Venice Biennale and Documenta at Kassel have been regular events for some time. But contemporary art in Britain is relatively unknown and generally unloved. At a time when greater and greater numbers in America, Germany, Holland and Japan are seeing more and more shows, the audience here is small and poorly served.

So the presence in London of a show of 145 recent paintings by 38 artists from six different countries was doubly unexpected. And for the two months it was on, it really did seem that London was the centre of the contemporary art world. Major critics, important dealers, committed collectors and artists travelled from all over Europe and America to visit the Royal Academy. Reviews appeared in every important art journal and every magazine and newspaper with a serious art column, even in countries without a national in the show.

The generally unsympathetic reaction of critics in this country caused Roberta Smith in an *Art in America* article to call it "the show the London art world loved to hate". Critics elsewhere found it the show they hated to love. After all, not even the Whitney and the Museum of Modern Art in New York, probably the world's greatest contemporary art museums in the world's undisputed contemporary art capital, have braved an international survey show of current work.

But New Spirit wasn't at Britain's most important showplace for contemporary art, the Tate, where an international survey show took place in 1964. Or even at the Hayward Gallery, which often houses shows organised in other countries and where a lacklustre survey show of recent sculpture called Pier and Ocean came and went in 1979 without leaving much of a trace. To everyone's astonishment, New Spirit appeared instead at the Royal Academy's Burlington House, Britain's 19th-century bastion of traditionalism. Not only did Christos Joachimides, Norman Rosenthal and Nicholas Serota have the awesome problem of choosing artists and particular works, but they also had to hang their choices without the flattering backdrop of pristine white walls and unobtrusive architecture in which contemporary art is normally enshrined.

On several different levels, this show demanded the cooperation of its audience, not least in attempting to understand its curators' notion of a new spirit in painting. Spirits are notably harder to define than Movements. Like all ambitious shows, it was entertaining, informative, puzzling and disappointing, in various combinations and sometimes all at once.

By the looks of things, "people and their emotions, landscapes and still-lives . . ." have indeed returned to "the centre of the argument of painting", as the show's Catalogue states they must. Assembled here was a collection of human images, landscapes and bird and animal studies not seen in a contemporary art show since the Salon des Refusés in 1874. Muhammad Ali, St. Francis, an Orientalist, the Lone Ranger, an unshaven arsonist, anonymous male and female nudes were together under the same roof with parrots, an eagle, a cormorant, camels, goats, horses, snakes, a rhinocerous, and views of Scottish countryside, German wasteland, a London park, Los Angeles drives and the South of France.

If canvases are again teeming with animal, vegetable and human life, they also seem charged with paint and colour once more. Even Andy Warhol has abandoned his deadpan renderings of soup cans and disasters for wildly coloured portraits of America's modern-day élite. His double-images here showed clearly how colour and brushwork operate on our impressions, changing the expression of the same silk-screened face from one canvas to another. Hockney, too, in his latest paintings has subjugated his masterful line to the power of bright, crudely applied colour, as if he had just discovered Matisse.

Whereas Warhol has only recently started 'painting', Hodgkin and Auerbach have pursued its possibilities throughout their careers. Compared with the apparently casual paintings of Warhol and Hockney, Hodgkin's are worked on almost to the point of no return. He spends several years on a single picture, applying his blocky shapes and lush colours one on top of another to create dense portraits and interiors that are layers of time as well as paint. In Auerbach's figure studies and mundane London landscapes, the paint is laid on so thick that all sense of the flat canvas underneath is lost. It hardly seems possible that his gloppy surfaces could be dry. The Italian Chia's rotond, folksy figures, contemporary kin of Chagall's peasants, slyly kiss, smoke and break wind on stridently coloured, tormented surfaces, the likes of which haven't been seen since Van Gogh. Obviously, as Christos Joachimides says, "the artists' studios are full of paint pots again".

Even artists who have formerly expressed themselves in other media have found the paintbrush and palette irresistible. Until about 1973, Merz made three-dimensional structures, of which the most well known is the igloo shape. Then he began to paint on unstretched canvas and with the wild animals exhibited here, which first appeared in New York last year, has concentrated on the painted image. Calzolari and Kounnelis are also Italian artists who are now making autonomous paintings after years of performance and conceptual art. Here in England, Bruce McLean has also recently started using paint, after performing regularly with his group, Nice Style, and others in the '70s. This was a first showing for his new paintings, quick-handed, glossy gestures on paper, like a shell game in paint. In his wacky compositions, faces are masks, tiny archetypal figures pose, tumble and tightrope walk, a white shoe nuzzles a bleary-eyed jug.

Since Abstract Expressionism and Colour Field, painting has been deliberately drained of such spontaneity and appeal to the emotions. From Pop Art to Photorealism to Minimal Art, it was an intellectual and technical exercise in restraint.

The evidence in this show suggests that not since the '20s and '30s has there been so much painted exposition of personal confusion and private concerns. It seems the Me Generation has produced artists who are once more romantic figures, lonely heroes anxiously attempting to embrace and comprehend the chaos of existence. Art is again a slice of life, instead of Olympian contemplation.

The prototypes of the romantic hero artist in this show, Guston, Morley and Schnabel, are of three different generations, but, interestingly, all are American. (Morley was born in England, but his physical and spiritual home has long been in the New World and America can rightfully claim him as her own.) Though Guston's very early paintings were figurative and full of social concern, he made his artistic reputation as an abstract expressionist. In the late '60s, he stopped making his graceful abstractions and began a series of uncouth, often auto-biographical paintings that continued until his death last year. Like garbage dumps for bad feelings, his canvases are littered with hairy knobbly-kneed legs, hooded figures, old shoes, booze bottles, half-smoked cigarettes and himself as a potato-head with a staring, bloodshot eye; crude, cartoon-like images outlined heavily in black but filled in lusciously with urgent pinks and reds. It's a testimony to Guston's superb painthandling that such unpalatable images can make such marvellous paintings.

Morley, too, seems to have a sense of urgency, constantly setting new challenges for himself and dazzling us with his fancy brushwork as he rises to them. Considered a founding father of Photorealism, he began to pull apart his photo-like images in the late '60s, finally abandoning them altogether for the exotic pictures in his imagination. He is the Lonely Ranger in his painting in this show, and the Long Ranger too, passing through many lands and tirelessly reporting on the confusion of vegetation, animal life and human activity he sees.

Schnabel is the upstart of this trio, a young New York artist whose outsized, muscle-bound pictures have taken the international art world by storm. With ham-fisted ferocity, he roughs esoteric figures and images on to cheap velvet and canvas encrusted with broken crockery, rude truths in a junky world. Schnabel is the youngest artist in the show, but his best paintings have a grandeur and maturity that make him look the outstanding painter of his generation.

Given their notion of a Spirit rather than a Movement, it was inevitable that the curators would ignore demarcations of age, style and nationality. The 38 artists in the show consisted of 11 Germans, nine Americans, eight Britons, five Italians, three Frenchmen, one Dane and one Chilean who has worked mainly in France and America. After 30 years of American dominance of mainstream contemporary art, it surprised almost everyone that Americans made up less than a quarter of the show. But, with the reappearance of their expressionist tradition, the Germans' weighty presence wasn't surprising at all. Many of them were seen in London for the first time, and one of them, Fetting, afterwards had successful first gallery shows in London and New York, a rare turnabout of the normal commercial gallery-museum relationship. Although he hasn't yet moved much beyond his '20s forerunners, Fetting's lurid colours and dense, matte surfaces, achieved through the use of powder paint, stood out from the work of most of his compatriots here. Hodicke's paintings were less memorable, presenting human figures against such murky, closed-in horizons that his exterior backgrounds seemed more like stuffy interiors. It was also a first showing of Keifer's work, which, once one's eyes became accustomed to the gloom, revealed layer upon layer of colour and shade. In fact, what at first seemed sinister eventually became

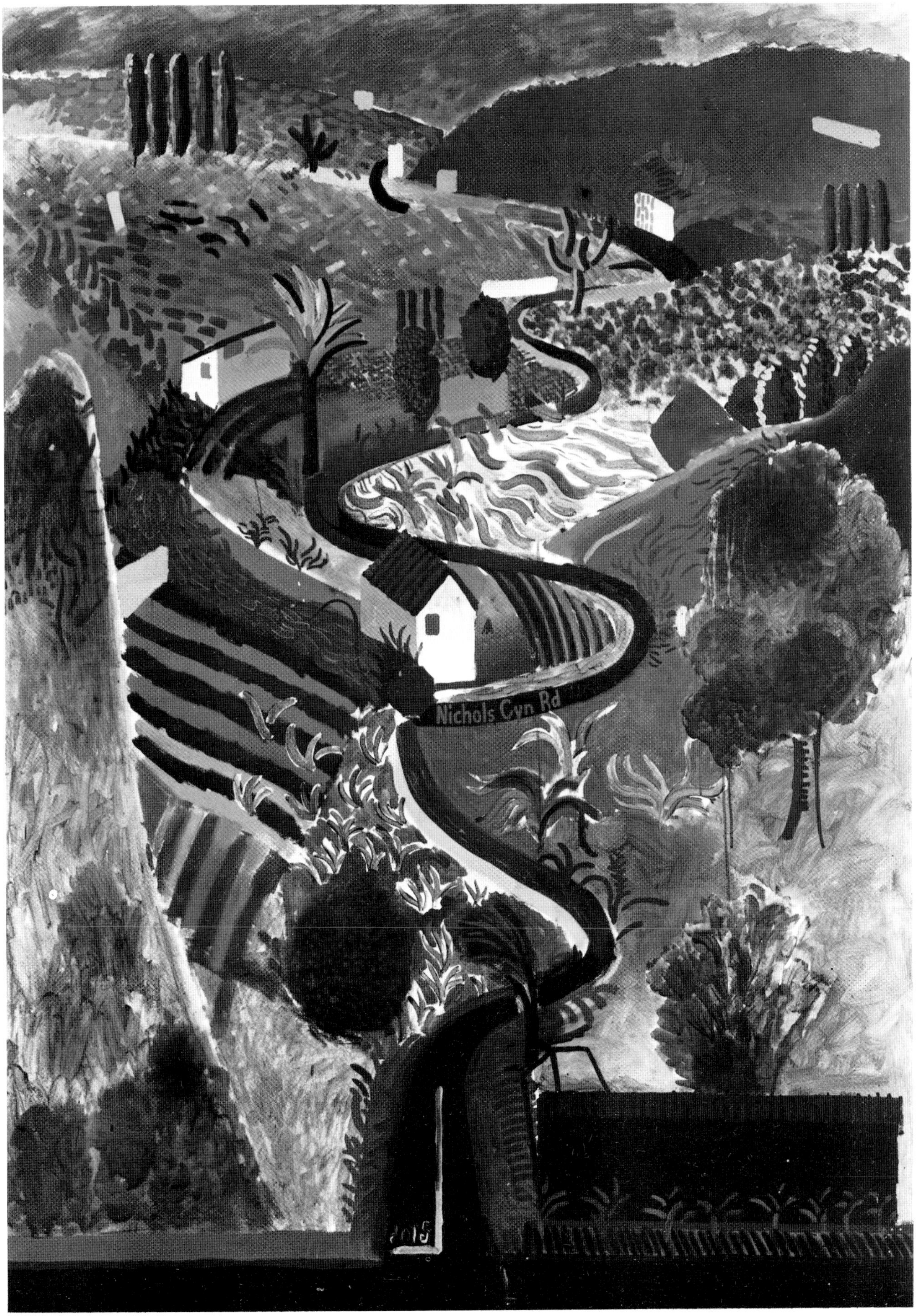

David Hockney *Nichols Canyon*

Matta *Leonardando Vinci*

Pablo Picasso   *Seated Old Man with Hat*

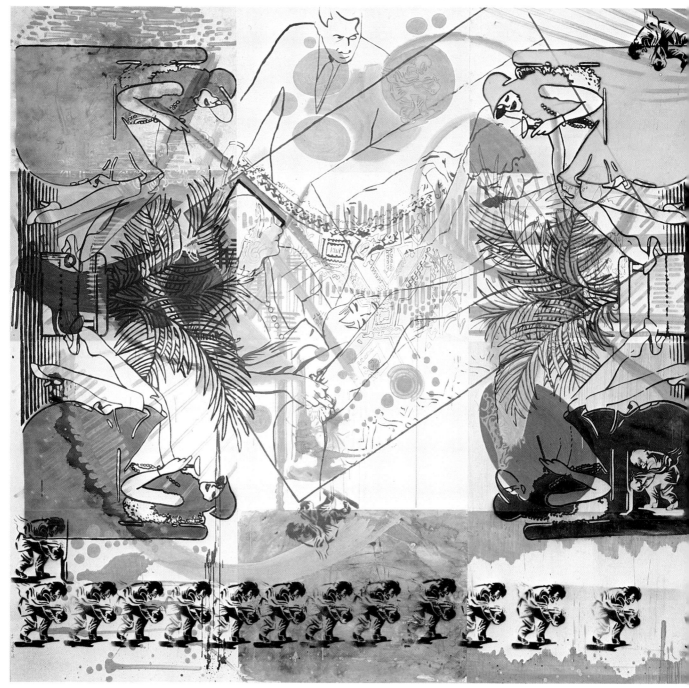

Sigmar Polke   *Kandisdingsda*

engaging. The tanks drawn up around the palette in *Painting Dispute* had the air of armoured creatures of the veldt, sniffing the breeze around a watering hole. Is that a pale, dead artist stretched out in the foreground? No, he's only sleeping and the painting is his dream.

In the Italian contingent, Chia and Paladino represented a large group of interesting New Wave compatriots, some of them more interesting than Paladino, who have brought about a mini-renaissance in Italy, the first since the Futurists' brief glory early this century.

It was revealing that the state of contemporary art in France is such that her two living representatives, Balthus and Helion, are 69 and 77 respectively.

Of the English group, Bacon, of course, has made his mark internationally, also Hockney and, to a lesser extent, Kitaj. But Hodgkin, Auerbach and Freud have up to now been honoured mainly by their own. Howard Hodgkin speaks for other artists when he talks of the burden he feels of fulfilling the increased expectations of his audience with each new group of paintings. Under a constant bombardment of information, the quantity and quality of our attention is often strained beyond its limits, and it becomes all too easy to pass over the familiar, mistaking novelty for innovation. So it takes a powerful committment to carry on, hoping people will continue to "see" the work if there are no radical changes in it. Hodgkin, Auerbach and Freud are artists whose apparently modest performance comes of conviction in the face of fashion and in the context of this show look most clearly like men whose time has come. Lucien Freud's full-frontal portraits are so loaded with meaty detail that they're almost unbearable to look at. The luminescence of the skin on his fleshy figures resembles the bloom of decay and the onlooker is face to face with his own mortality.

The most disparate bunch in the show was the Americans. In a room by himself and a class of his own was Twombly. It is incredible that this was his first museum appearance in London and regrettable that visitors to the show who'd never seen his work before didn't get to see some of his monumental paintings on canvas. Since the '50s, Twombly has expressed with his ethereal doodles some kind of universal preoccupation and, at the same time, redefined the rudiments of composition. He's claimed a territory for his own and it's hard to see a scrabbled line or scribbled word on canvas without thinking the artist is trespassing on Twombly's ground.

In proving that painting isn't dead, killed off by Conceptualism and Per-formance, this show acknowledged its debt to a few true believers who knew it all along. There were six of them here, Picasso, Guston, de Kooning, Balthus, Helion and Matta, the Patriarchs of the show. In his rightful place at its heart was Picasso, whose titanic efforts made so much of the work that surrounded him here possible. He, more than any other artist here, exemplified the precepts of the show, an artist who loved the paintbrush, painted what he felt and looked at everything. Of the others, Matta and Helion seemed firmly rooted to the past, whereas Balthus, Guston and de Kooning looked like masters of the present. It was amusing to mentally rehang Guston's *Talking* next to Chia's *Che Fuma*, de Kooning's *Untitled II* next to McLean's *Two Ties* and Balthus's *Reclining Nude* next to Hockney's *Portrait of Divine*.

In several cases, the curators capitalised on stylistic differences to create some informative groupings. At the start of the show, Penck's black and white calligraphy seemed a comedown, faced off as it was against Morley's brightly coloured figurations. But after a moment, his fat, dark strokes began to combine to make little pictures and his canvases became hunting grounds for enigmatic images. Is that a cross at the head of a grave in the lower righthand corner of *Atomicon* or a stick figure person with outstretched arms doing a sit up? In the middle of *XXX* is the arrow with a truncated shaft beneath five rows of dots the stem of a flower, a preacher exhorting his congregation or an arrow with a truncated shaft?

In the great hall, occupying pride of place in the galleries, and possibly in the curators' affections, were the Frenchman Balthus, the American de Kooning and the German Baselitz. Balthus was honoured with seven large paintings, a homage that for many was long overdue. He is now an old man, taking his pleasure in paint, enjoying the maddening poise of beautiful young girls, serenely, as only an old man can.

de Kooning has always been more exuberant and refuses to settle down. In his '50s paintings of women, among the wildly stroked patches of colour, are brazen bright red lips, open legs and fleshy thighs. All through the cool years of American contemporary art, he carried on his high-spirited love affair with paint, tempering his rowdiness with perfect taste.

Balthus and de Kooning meet in a rather dry fusion in Baselitz, who in the '70s tried to cut his human figures loose from illusion by standing them on their heads. But the results look more like a pedantic exercise than a liberation.

Possibly the most surprising combination, and the most successful, was Stella face to face with Marden. Stella led the way to Minimal Art in the '60s with paintings of narrow, parallel bands of white on a black ground. When, in the mid-70's, he made the first of his three-dimensional metal constructions, the man who was once dismissed by a critic as the "pin stripe boy" became the carnival king. His swooping, soaring shapes and raucous colours have all the joy and fury of a good-natured riot. Withstanding their assault in dreamy silence were Marden's three-panel paintings in offbeat blues. His many-layered encaustic surfaces, that seem to draw in light and play it back softened and diffused, and his deft juxtaposition of Cezannesque colours made him by 1970 one of the key artists in American contemporary art. By 1973, he'd had a retrospective at the Guggenheim in New York, but his presence in this show was his first appearance in Britain and pointed up the sad lack of opportunity here to see important contemporary artists.

In the end, the differences the curators emphasised, and the ones they didn't, required a tremendous effort of assimilation in order to see the show as a whole. But once that effort was made, what initially looked like 'anything goes' began to seem like 'all things are possible'. For young British painters who see so little of the exciting art being·made elsewhere, except in art magazines, that's a particularly vital message.

Of course, everyone with a serious interest in art is a surrogate curator, mentally creating The Perfect Show. Of the artists not here, strong cases have been made by many for Jasper Johns and Neil Jenney. And among the candidates for inclusion were two women who seemed such obvious choices that some called their omission sexism on the part of the curators. Agnes Martin's spare 'landscapes' of pencil lines delicately ruled on blank canvas were some of the first and most beautiful minimal paintings of the '60s. After giving up painting in the late '60s, she re-emerged in 1975 with a series of canvases washed with limpid colour that are amongst the most lyrical paintings produced in the last five years. When, in the mid-70s, Jennifer Bartlett abandoned painting systematically arranged dots on strict groups of same-sized metal plates for a primitive, personal imagery, she was one of the first artists to lead the way out of the 'painting is dead' cul-de-sac that Minimal and Conceptual Art had produced.

Of the artists who were in the show, it was disappointing to see that Polke's recent paintings were less interesting than his work in the '60s and that Matta's work was no more interesting now than it was then. Hacker appeared here to live up to his name and Lupertz was represented by better paintings in a recent Whitechapel show. On the evidence of the works shown here, Koberling, Graubner, Kirkeby and Charlton were out of their depth. Ryman, whose variations on a theme of white are some of the most eloquent paintings of the last 20 years, was ill-served by the Royal Academy's dado and cream hessian-covered walls. Bacon and Richter were ill-served by paintings that were below their best. But, on the basis that controversy is better than no comment, what were seen by some as the show's flaws proved as informative as its successes.

Over 78,000 people saw A New Spirit in Painting, more than double the combined numbers for the Jasper Johns, Ellsworth Kelly and Pier and Ocean shows. Assuming that almost everyone in London who is seriously interested in contemporary art saw those shows, it's clear that many of those who saw New Spirit were there as devotees of the Royal Academy and weren't prepared for what was inside. Judging by several comments overheard in the galleries, it was, for some, an alarming experience. But there must have been many others who didn't know about contemporary Art, but, as a result of this show, now like what they know. Hopefully, 78,000 attendances will serve as a pointer to future possibilities.

Recently, the *New York Times* announced on its Art Page "... a change is upon us in the form of an energetic wave of neo-Expressionist painting. This is an astonishing development." Who could have foreseen that news of that development would appear first in the venerable halls of the Royal Academy, Britain's genteel doyenne of conservatism.

Less than a year after its close, it looks like A New Spirit in Painting has the makings of a landmark show.

DORIS SAATCHI

Treasures From Chatsworth

The exhibition Treasures from Chatsworth which was so beautifully mounted in the Royal Academy gave my family and myself enormous pleasure. Prior to its being shown in Burlington House it had been on an extensive tour of the United States. Owing to the fact that the exhibition coincided with the time Chatsworth was closed to the public, I was able to add some extra works of art taken from the public route which, since they were already on display, it was not possible to include when it toured America.

The works of art shown in the marvellous rooms in Burlington House represent the accretion of pictures, books, jewellery and plate amassed over the last 300 years. Although they are all now housed at Chatsworth, in former times they were more diffusely spread, some in Devonshire House which used to stand in Piccadilly almost opposite the Ritz Hotel, others in Lord Burlington's villa at Chiswick, and some at Hardwick Hall, the house now belonging to the National Trust formerly owned by my family.

Before writing about the works of art themselves, perhaps I should say a word or two about the house. Originally there was an Elizabethan house on the exact site of the present house built by the redoubtable Bess of Hardwick towards the end of the 16th century. Roughly a hundred years later the 4th Earl, who was to become the 1st Duke, started to rebuild it. Although externally there is nothing to be seen of Bess's Chatsworth, inside there are still brickwork and beams of her house. For example, the medicine cupboard in my wife's bathroom is divided by an Elizabethan beam. The 4th Earl started his work about 1685 and the square block of the house was finished in 1707, the year that he died. Then in the first half of the 19th century the 6th Duke added the wing which stretches north from the main block. It is interesting that for many years this wing was regarded as an architectural outrage and indeed my father toyed with the idea of pulling it down. Architectural fashion changes as all other fashions. It is now regarded as a fine example of late Regency architecture and if I were to try and lay a finger on it there would be an enormous outcry.

To turn now to the exhibits. I have mentioned Hardwick and two of the earliest things on show were Hobbes's manuscript and a miniature portrait of the philosopher. He was tutor to the 2nd and 3rd Earls of Devonshire and spent much of his time there. There is an old wives' tale that his ghost is to be seen walking in the park at Hardwick the night before the head of my family is to die. I do not believe in this, but all the same should get a bit worried if I were told at breakfast one day that the ghost of Hobbes had been seen at Hardwick the previous night.

The 4th Earl was created a Duke by William and Mary as a result of his support for their cause as opposed to that of James II. My family owes a great deal to William and Mary. Quite apart from creating the dukedom the sovereigns were extremely generous. In the exhibition there were a number of gifts from them to the 1st Duke, fine examples of Dutch Delft tulip vases, and a really magnificent dressing-table service, almost certainly a present from the King and Queen as it bears their coat of arms. I think that this dressing-table set, with one possible exception, is of the most exquisite craftsmanship of anything in the exhibition. Also from the 1st Duke's time is a really magnificent silver chandelier that hangs in the State Rooms at Chatsworth. Unfortunately it was not possible to include it in the exhibition.

Chatsworth is indeed fortunate in its collection of plate, the crowning glory being the solid gold ewer and dish by Pierre Platel from the early 17th century. This is normally on loan to the Victoria and Albert Museum. Two years or so ago it was on loan to another exhibition when the ewer was stolen. It caused all concerned great anxiety, the danger being that, as it is of pure gold, it could be melted down and sold for its worth in that metal. Fortunately all was well and the ewer was recovered.

The silver-gilt specimens are very beautiful. Outstanding are two very fine Pilgrim bottles of approximately the same date as the dressing-table set I referred to. They bear the 1st Duke's coat of arms, and it interests me very much why these bottles were reproduced in precious metals as works of art. They are copied from the leather bottles attached to the saddle of those who went on pilgrimages in earlier times. No doubt experts in this field will know the reason for their reproduction but to me it remains a mystery.

To turn now to what probably is considered to be the crowning glory of the works of art at Chatsworth – its collection of drawings. Broadly speaking, these fall into two categories, the first a large collection of Old Master drawings accumulated by the 2nd Duke. These include a number of Rembrandt landscapes, some beautiful drawings by Rubens, a Leonardo da Vinci and several Raphaels, together with a large number of great Italian Renaissance draughtsmen. Of all the drawings my favourite is the Rubens of the girl with the milkchurn. In the unlikely event of my having been a Pharaoh, I would certainly have had this drawing buried with me. Not only is the drawing beautifully executed but it has a marvellous feeling of peace and tranquillity. The Rembrandts are exquisite drawings and what always impresses me about them is how in a really very small space, eight inches by six, he could draw a landscape that gives one an impression of great space, breadth and width, a truly astonishing achievement.

The other section of drawings is those by Inigo Jones, that remarkable man who was Clerk of the Works to James I and Charles I. Particularly under the latter he designed many stage costumes and theatrical sets for the masques that were so popular at Court. These give a unique insight into the great master's skill and were acquired by the 3rd Earl of Burlington. They were inherited by his daughter who married the 4th Duke of Devonshire, and so came into the collection.

To turn now to the paintings. My family's collection of works of art is strong in this field. Again we must be grateful to Lord Burlington for the marvellous pictures my family inherited from him. After my father's death we were faced with severe problems of raising money to pay death duties and to my lasting regret we had to part with the crowning glory of the paintings, the triptych by Memling. Happily it is in the National Gallery. Also we had to part with one of the three Rembrandts, *The Philosopher*. However, let me not be churlish. There is still at Chatsworth a fine collection of paintings ranging over several centuries, the best of which were on display at the exhibition. Indeed it was strengthened by the addition of two paintings by Franz Hals and one by Rembrandt. These pictures normally hang in that part of the house through which the public passes so it was not possible to send them to America. As I have said, fortunately the exhibition at the Royal Academy coincided with the time of year when the house was shut and it was therefore possible to add these three masterpieces. Two of the Rembrandts on view are both well known and have been exhibited in many parts of the world. It would be impertinent for me to comment on their respective quality. Though *King Uzziah Stricken with Leprosy* is perhaps better known, my preference is for the *Portrait of an Old Man*. The painting of the skin, so clearly that of a very old man, is a truly miraculous achievement. Of the two Hals's one was acquired through Lord

Burlington and the other probably bought by the 3rd Duke of Devonshire. They make a fine pair. They are shown in the Statue Gallery at Chatsworth flanking *King Uzziah* and they do make a very splendid group of pictures. These are part of the essential contents of Chatsworth that have now been leased for 99 years to the charitable trust I set up to maintain Chatsworth for at least, I hope, some decades ahead. So they are safe and all being well will remain at Chatsworth for the next 98 years.

The next two pictures I would like to comment on are the two Nicholas Poussins, *The Holy Family* and *Et in Arcadia Ego*. Since the exhibition, *The Holy Family* has been sold to provide funds for the charitable trust to which I have just alluded. The choice was a difficult one. The major consideration was that the work of art had to come from the private part of the house since, should it have been taken from the public route, it might well be that someone had come many many miles to see the picture only to find it had been sold. I hope the choice was right. Certainly the money it raised at auction will go a long way, but by no means all the way, to provide the necessary finance for the charitable trust. The other Poussin, *Et in Arcadia Ego*, is my favourite of the entire collection. It has got a magic quality about it. It is also, I understand, of great importance that it is the last picture that Poussin painted in the romantic style before he moved towards the style of *The Holy Family*.

I think the most romantic part of the exhibition was the room in which Lord Burlington, painted by Knapton, gazed down the room looking over some of the finest pictures he collected. There is the Velasquez, *Portrait of a Lady in a Mantilla*. There is a certain query as to the authenticity of this painting and some experts in this country are not convinced. However, when some years ago it was sent to an exhibition of the artist's work in Madrid the authorities there had no doubt about its authenticity. There is the Murillo, *The Holy Family*, and although I am not very fond of religious pictures, I make an exception of this one. Its air of domesticity and tranquillity to me says something very special. Then comes de Vos's enchanting *Portrait of a Little Girl*, possibly his own daughter. This lovely picture is reproduced in postcards sold at Chatsworth and it is probably the most popular buy of all the reproductions.

Of the three Van Dyck's in the exhibition the full-length portrait of Arthur Goodwin is outstanding. It is, I believe, generally regarded as one of his finest works. The other two smaller portraits are very charming. They are of Charles Cavendish, second son of the 2nd Earl of Devonshire, and Lucius Cary, 2nd Viscount Falkland.

Nicholas Poussin *The Shepherds in Arcadia*

E leur donray tresgrant finance .
Silz en scauent venir a chief .
Maistre alphons pmier medecin .
Se vostre mal nest par trop grief .
Incontinent vous guarrons .

Vaspasien .

Approuchies si vous monstrerons .
Le mal qui si fort nous trauaille .

Le .ij. medicin en
regardant son visaige .

Ha maistre alphons vecy merueille .

audier et conforter le boulsist. Et en telle fa
chon quentendre povez estoit grand de trasignies
prisonnier ou chastel de victruse duquel pour le
present nous bous lairons le parler Jusques heure
soit dy retourner pour bous racompter des fais
et baillances de messire gillion de trasignies son pe

Comment hertan combatit le roy haldin. Com
ment il le desconfit. Et du mariage de messire
gillion de trasignies. Puis parle de la grant et
criminele bataille qui fut deuant babilonne
ou messire gillion desconfit les sarrazins. Et de sa
main occist le roy de mobrant
y dessus est assez plainnement declaire
la maniere et comment messire gil
lion de trasignies fut prisonnier en

Georgiana Countess Spencer
Daughter of Stephen Poyntz Esq.

Thomas Gainsborough   *Georgiana Poyntz, Countess Spencer*

Pompeo Batoni   *William Cavendish, Fifth Duke of Devonshire*   *Treasures from Chatsworth*

Inigo Jones *A Star Masquer*

Rembrandt Van Rijn   *Portrait of an Old Man*

To turn now to the 18th-century paintings of Sir Joshua Reynolds. Chatsworth is very fortunate in having a group of three family portraits by him, a sketch of Lady Spencer and her baby daughter Georgiana, another of Georgiana when Duchess of Devonshire, and the great painting of Georgiana and her baby daughter. It is fascinating that we have three generations of the same family by the same artist. Although perhaps I would prefer to keep Poussin's *Et in Arcadia Ego*, if things got really bad it would be the picture of Georgiana and her baby that I would hold on to as long as possible. There is also a sketch of Georgiana's mother by Gainsborough which is a fine picture which hangs prominently in the private part of the house at Chatsworth. Then there is Sir Joshua's portrait of the 5th Duke's second wife, Lady Elizabeth Foster. To round off the family group there is the Batoni of the 5th Duke, so that particular part of my family tree is very well represented. Georgiana's son, the 6th Duke, was shown in a portrait by Sir Edwin Landseer. It is a charming picture of the Duke in his box at the opera. This is slightly unexpected as all his life he suffered from deafness. He was a great admirer of Landseer's work and we are lucky to have two of his major paintings.

The 6th Duke was a passionate collector. Among his major additions to the works of art at Chatsworth were books. His taste was eclectic. If I have a regret about the exhibition, and the fault is entirely mine, I feel the 6th Duke's contribution to the collections was not given sufficient prominence.

We now come to the pictures that I have added to the collection. They do not of course measure up in quality to the masterpieces collected by my family. However, I am reasonably satisfied that they are a worthwhile addition to the Chatsworth collection, particularly the portraits by Lucian Freud of my family and his outstanding work, *Large Interior, London, W.9*. I also added the two really splendid Samuel Palmers and, although they were painted late in his career when his work was generally considered to be less important than in his early days, they are two lovely works of art and do look very well, hung at Chatsworth. There is also the charming Degas drawing of a horse which hangs next to Susan Crawford's splendid portrait of my great race mare, Park Top, with Lester Piggott in the saddle. It is a matter of considerable satisfaction to me that not only did I buy the Degas but also a number of other pictures from the mare's winnings.

Although Chatsworth has a great library, the books, because they are not easy to show to advantage, were not strongly represented. There was the manuscript, *Elements of Law*, by Thomas Hobbes. Henry VII's prayer book or *Book of Hours* which he gave to his daughter, later to become James IV of Scotland's queen, is a really lovely illuminated manuscript and is made romantic by the inscriptions which Henry VII wrote in it to his daughter:

"Remembre yor kynde and lovyng fader in yor prayers.

Henry Kᵧ."

and

"Pray for your lovyng fader that gave you thys book and I geve you att all tymes godds blessȳg and myne.

Henry Kᵧ."

The missal came into my family's possession in a curious way. Lord Burlington, a skilled architect, built a house for a General Wade in Piccadilly which no longer stands. In return General Wade gave him this precious book. Also of interest among the books shown was the earliest book written in English on architecture by John Shute. This must surely have come through Lord Burlington with his passion for architecture. Other books on view were a number of early 19th-century illustrated flower books. Rather unexpectedly Chatsworth library was weak in this field, and through my trustees I was lucky enough to acquire in the early 1970's a number of very fine volumes depicting flowers and vegetables and thus fill a hole in the collection. The ones in the exhibition were Pierre-Joseph Redouté's *Les Roses*, Samuel Curtis's *The Beauties of Flora*, and Jan and Caspar Commelins' *Horti Medici Amstelodamensis Rariorum Plantarum Descriptio et Icones*.

Now a brief word on the furniture shown. Of greatest interest is one of a pair of marvellous library tables made for Lord Burlington. They look very well at Chatsworth in one of the main corridors. Also shown were three of a set of seven splendid silk-covered gilded chairs by Kent, and a splendid seaweed marquetry chest from the 1st Duke's day.

That covers the main objects shown in the exhibition, except for a number of oddities: Henry VIII's boxwood rosary possibly carved from designs by Holbein, the Kniphausen "Hawk" of the 17th century (it is unknown how it came into my family) and then the really beautiful watch and châtelaine almost certainly made for Georgiana, although the initials included in the piece are a little confusing. It is an exquisite piece of craftsmanship. Even more personal in their association with my family are the charming letters written to the 6th Duke by Dickens and Thackeray.

The exhibition shows the breadth and scope of the Treasures of Chatsworth and I profoundly hope they will remain there for many years to come.

DEVONSHIRE

Leonardo da Vinci

Paul Storr   *Candelabrum*

Adriaen Kocks *Delft tulip vase*

Johann Zoffany   *The Children of the Fourth Duke of Devonshire*

Treasures from Chatsworth

Honoré Daumier

What is it about a collection of lithographs of ordinary unknown French people of the last century that should have attracted such large and enthusiastic crowds to the Royal Academy earlier this year? This was the response to the exhibition of part of the Armand Hammer Daumier Collection. In its entirety this collection consists of more than 4,000 lithographs and woodcuts, various bound periodicals, oil paintings, watercolours, drawings, bronzes and even an original lithographic stone all by the 19th-century artist, Honoré Daumier. Since Daumier left us the largest number of visual images created by any artist up to the end of the last century the scope of the collection is not surprising, but the delighted and amused reaction it inspires in 1981 is perhaps more so. As a caricaturist myself I am very well aware of the power of humour, and it is Daumier's brilliant and irreverent use of satire to make a point that I believe evokes such an instant and knowing response in his audience.

It is in the drawings themselves that the humour lies, the captions are very rarely what make us laugh and indeed were usually provided by Daumier's editor, and a mere description of the subject matter of one of his lithographs would give no idea of just how funny it might be. To say for instance that one of my favourites shows "a couple staring at the night sky" will illustrate the problem of conveying in words the subtlety and humour with which he manages to endow the simplest subject. Perhaps it is partly the joy of recognising something in ourselves that gives us such great pleasure in these apparently simple themes. To take that particular drawing as an example, all of us at one time or another must have gazed upwards to the stars and felt strongly our own insignificance in the face of such vast and impenetrable mysteries. To see the almost child-like innocence of this very ordinary and somewhat unattractive couple in their fruitless search for the planet "Leverrier" makes us laugh at our own ridiculous predicament as human beings aspiring to the unattainable knowledge of the infinite. But we laugh affectionately, and indeed this sympathetic attitude to his victim seems to run through most of Daumier's social cartoons. This is not to say that he does not observe and condemn the foolishness of the human condition, but he does at least seem to understand and forgive. This use of humour as a gentle weapon is very different from my own and, although there are obviously many aspects in which as a caricaturist I find myself using an approach similar to his, in this particular way I feel we differ quite strongly. I tend to be unsympathetic to the people I draw, to use laughter against the side of man that I despise – his cruelty, his greed, and above all his misuse of power.

Perhaps it is in Daumier's drawings of lawyers and the "vile body of the legislature" that we come closest to each other in our approach. Here he conveys brilliantly exactly the sort of misuse of power that I find so appalling: there are countless lithographs depicting the greed and lack of integrity of some of the members of this profession – barristers squeezing money out of impoverished clients to take on cases they know they have little chance of winning; accepting briefs they know to be immoral for the sake of their fee; pleading with all the skills of an actor a cause with which they may have no sympathy. Daumier worked for a process-server for a while in his youth, an experience which he hated and which no doubt made him well aware of the potentially painful results of being taken to court.

In these legal drawings, as in most of his work, Daumier uses the unreality of caricature to convey a very real point. Just as an impressionist is most successful and can give us most insight into his subject when he exaggerates various carefully chosen aspects, so a caricaturist can inspire a quick and direct response in his audience by stretching a face, expression, or even position of the body. Like Daumier, I first found a sympathetic setting for this type of work in a new magazine, in my case "Private Eye", in his "La Caricature". It can be of enormous support to find oneself surrounded for perhaps the first time by others sympathetic to one's way of thought, and I suspect that in both these periodicals Daumier and I found a similar sense of irreverence and satire which gave us the freedom to explore the possibilities of our talents in a creative atmosphere.

There is great pleasure for the caricaturist in carrying his audience with him – educating them in his style if you like. When I draw a politician for the first time, for instance, I will probably only stretch his features a limited amount; it takes time for me to "dare" to pull his or her face out of reality. Sometimes I can successfully continue this process over a series of drawings until ultimately I reach purely a symbol of the person and yet which contains all the essential qualities of my subject. When I have taken a face this far, however, it obviously becomes difficult for the viewer to recognise without having followed my "path of discovery". I see less of this fascination with caricature for its own sake in Daumier's social cartoons but in his political drawings, particularly those of Louis-Philippe, our styles seem to be more closely linked. In some of these he has reduced the king to a simple pear without any features at all: this was doubly useful as in vernacular French a "pear" is a "dolt" or "dope". It also helped to protect him against prosecution – to take him to court for having ridiculed an apparently anonymous piece of fruit would have been patently absurd. It was important for Daumier to minimise his chances of being prosecuted; he had already spent nearly three months in prison the previous year for producing various scandalous drawings of the king. In the first of these drawings he employs a device which also shows a link in our approach and one which I tend to use myself: the conveying of a thought or idea in an instantly forceful way by the use of the functions of the body as a symbol. Thus in the drawing we see a gigantic Louis-Philippe having his hideously gaping mouth literally stuffed with tributes while at the same time a shower of medals pours from his anus. It is perhaps interesting that a century later in this so-called "permissive society" I have always had similar difficulty in finding a place to print such drawings and have indeed been threatened with prosecution on a small number of occasions without, thank God, having to endure the prison sentence that he did. The fear of censorship haunted his work from this time on, and indeed probably accounts for the very small number of political cartoons that Daumier produced in comparison to the more harmless social satires.

Whereas I prefer to draw on well-known recognisable subjects for my caricatures – political and public figures and so on – Daumier's most successful work is of ordinary, unknown people. He drew entirely from memory, and even felt that to draw from Nature tended to interfere with the purity of his thought. Certainly this produces no lack of sincerity in his portraits. He must have had the most acute powers of observation and retention to enable him to reproduce in his studio such extremely life-like and believable subjects. I find television and photographs very useful in refreshing my visual memory and I also try to make sketches from life whenever I can but, as with Daumier, the real work goes on inside my head.

As it is forbidden to sketch in the House of Commons without special permission, I find political party conferences and Trade Union assemblies very useful occasions for making working drawings of politicians and trade unionists to act as guiding notes for the basis of caricatures. In Daumier's day too it was difficult to draw politicians in session but, when he was commisioned to produce a series of bronze figures of the leading deputies of the Conservative party, he was forced to find a way round it and this time at least to take his inspiration direct from life. It is said he smuggled pieces of clay into the Chamber and, hardly glancing down at the faces he was producing, worked them by feel with his hands safely hidden by the seat in front. These sketches in clay have the most marvellous immediacy and life to them and are among my favourite examples of his work.

As with any great artist, the more one attempts to describe the value and significance of his work the less able one will be to convey its true achievement. By definition a work of art is successful if it conveys something that one cannot put into words, but there is perhaps one attribute that may be fairly said to apply to all such successful art of whatever type and that is the quality of being at once strongly rooted in its own time and yet timeless. This is most certainly true of the work of Daumier – the characters we see in the lithographs are so completely of their own period, accurately bringing to life a particular street scene, court room or bedroom of 19th-century France and yet also showing us feelings and situations with which we can totally identify in 1981. A lithograph like *A Disturbed Night*, for instance, shows a father airing a nappy by the open fire while the mother tries to quieten a screaming baby on the bed. We feel a strong sense of period and of how family life must have been at that time and in that type of room, and yet it will evoke just as strong a reaction in any parent as if it had been drawn today. Human emotions re-main unchanged in spite of the advent of disposable nappies and central heating . . .

The Academy exhibition included a small number of Daumier's oil paintings and water colours. Painting was his great love, and he possessed a brilliant talent in this more "serious" field that went largely unrecognised in his lifetime. To feed himself and his family he was forced to produce an astonishing number of the humorous cartoons that the public demanded. These were sold over the counter at the rate of two or three new lithographs each week, but whenever he had the chance he would escape to his painting. He produced some sensitive and beautiful works, among which are a large number depicting Don Quixote and Sancho Panza – a subject that has always fascinated artists, myself included, for its romantic and yet humorous qualities. I was delighted to find one of these included at the Academy.

Daumier was only too well aware of the insincerity and ludicrous posturing of many art critics and "connoisseurs" and indeed made many very funny lithographs on this theme, but he was a man who much appreciated genuine and unforced enjoyment of his work. I am sure he would have been delighted to know that not only were his lithographs giving the public as much pleasure in 1981 as they did when originally produced, but that he was also now accepted as a "serious" artist whose paintings and sculptures were being shown the appreciation they deserve and which had been lacking in his own time.

GERALD SCARFE

Un Avocat Plaidant

Honoré Daumier

Don Quixote y Sancho Panza   *Honoré Daumier*

A Travers les Ateliers

Honoré Daumier

Painting From Nature

The Royal Academy's Summer Exhibition of Painting from Nature showed how artists developed the practice of taking not only their notebooks but their paints and canvases "into the field".

As Professor Gowing reminds us in his introduction to the catalogue, what was a sporadic habit in the 17th and 18th centuries became a creed in the 19th. Indeed, the habit, enlarged by the Realists, and given a great extension of spatial language by the Impressionists, has never really left us.

Landscape painting from nature may not receive much critical attention at present, but this does not prevent many full-time painters and thousands of Sunday painters from engaging their powers of *plein-air* observation.

But, because contemporary painting from nature is much practised and little critically regarded, two misconceptions have tended to grow up about it; one that it is comparatively easy and the other that it is comparatively unimaginative.

Plein-air painting may be an easy genre in which to perform badly, but since its inception it has been one of the most difficult in which to perform well. The reasons are not hard to seek.

Painters of the Renaissance, the Baroque and the Rococo were creating conceptions of landscape in terms of a well-stocked repertoire of pictorial devices and conventions. The simplifying, the ordering and the spatial and tonal organisation were those of the studio: the devices derived largely from a concern with organising figures in a contained setting. Even when painters came to work before the subject in the studio, they were doing so in a closely restricted space, usually in a limited range of light and shade, and with a contrived limitation of subject matter: this is still so.

But when the landscape painter stands before nature, he may have to organise five miles of space where the studio painter organises five yards: more dauntingly, he is faced, from the brightest light to the deepest shadow, with a range of tone vastly greater than he can begin to match with the whitest white and the blackest black of his palette.

If the studio painter must reinvent his tonal range, how much more must the landscape painter do so. Then there is the matter of the sky. How is this to be understood? Is it a back-cloth dropping behind the sky-line, or is it atmosphere coming to the artist's feet? The sky is his source of light, yet that small part of it which is to appear in his painting seldom is. But that very part may be the brightest tone of his subject. How is he to adjust to this seemingly intractable dilemma? The studio painter's binocular vision will normally serve his reading of space to his limits of distance; it serves no more than the nearest middle distance of a landscape. The *plein-air* painter must find other means of understanding depth, in atmospheric and colour recession and in differences of scale, though even these diminish in a geometrical curve into the distance.

Space creates another special problem in the depiction of landscape. Nature provides contrasts of shape no less than the studio, but the constituents of which these shapes are made, leaves, branches, twigs, bricks, rocks and blades of grass, have a tiresome habit of repeating themselves into landscape depth. A painter makes a mark for a leaf or a rock in the foreground. A smaller mark may represent a leaf or a rock a little further off. But in the near distance an individual leaf, an individual rock, can no longer be distinguished or counted, only clumps of leaves and heaps of rock. In the distance he can see only trees and hills.

How many different kinds of "count" does he take notice of into the distance, and most importantly how does he adjust the nature of his brushmarks to each different spatial meaning?

The old studio landscape painters did not altogether have to face this problem; the early Flemish landscapes, with all their beauty, have an affinity to scale models in which the detail of every constituent can be clearly distinguished. Even the Baroque often practised a compositional convention of foreground, middle distance and distance, leaping tonally into space with contrived alternations of light and dark, and essentially with a convention of mark and texture assigned to each.

But the painter before nature would defeat his purpose by taking refuge in such conventions (he put himself out-of-doors precisely in order to question such conventions), and so this language of marks remains one of his special difficulties.

Now all these particular difficulties of landscape arise from the fact that the solutions are not custom-built. The studio provides, or once provided, answers culled from traditions and conventions of simplifying and ordering.

When painters, with Constable in the van, first went right into the open to put down their unconditioned sensations of the real visual experience, they found nature offering no such ready answers.

And in this we find the reason why the idea that "Painting before Nature" is unimaginative is also a misconception. From Constable onwards the history of observed landscape is the history of painters forced to invent, each one for himself, a tradition of marks, conventions and simplifications which would answer his own sensations. What could more strongly exercise the pictorial imagination than this? Look at a typical range of Rococo painting of the 18th century. Of course, each considerable artist is recognisable by his individuality. But there is a family likeness in much of it which is born of those studio traditions to which painters still clung. An artist might seek eminence by being better within these traditions than his rival. But it is the characteristic of post-Constable landscape in the 19th century that the artist is not just seeking to be better but different. The work of every great master has been identifiable by the way in which it rises above tradition, but never before the 19th century had so many artists signed themselves without signature, by distinctive differences of language.

These differences were born of necessity before nature, not out of self-regard, of the need to invent in the face of problems for which few escape routes lay to hand. To invent a language of truth before nature is not an act of imitation but of high imagination, and it is little wonder that many fell by the wayside, or sought refuge in the debased academicism of the Salons.

One of the special values of the Royal Academy's Painting from Nature exhibition is that it revealed how painters first came to face the difficulties of their new experiments, and how they began to find a new language of the observant imagination to reach solutions.

Like all good exhibitions it was to be enjoyed for its own sake, and not merely for its didactics. But it is significant, and in its own way didactially valuable, that the exhibition did not extend to Impressionism. Nobody who cares for landscape would seek to diminish the achievement and importance of the Impressionists; but in the minds of an art-going public they have to some degree stolen the thunder of their predecessors. Painting from Nature did a service in reminding us how strongly the foundations had already been laid. By the time of Monet and Renoir at Argenteuil the landscape of sensation was no longer terra incognita, and painters of the sort whose work we saw in the Diploma Galleries had done much of the surveying.

Examples of the renowned names were present; Claude, Constable, Turner, Corot.

Claude represented himself, and the 17th century, in his *Landscape with a Goatherd*. Our familiarity with Claude's drawings of the Campagna may lead us to see this early expression of light and air as made, or anyway resolved, in the studio, though no lesser an authority than Constable thought it to have been painted before nature. Certainly Claude was, in the eyes of later painters, the great herald of luminous reality, and his example is none the less for having wound its way through the channels of Romanticism, notably to Turner.

Turner himself, in his *Thames near Walton Bridges* is altogether on the out-door spot, unusually even for himself; the truth of his tonality and mark-making response seems to owe nothing to the studio. In such panels as this Turner came as close as he ever did to Constable, whose *View towards the Rectory, East Bergholt* shows the same observed and inventive liberation from convention. Corot's *Basilica of Constantine*, with his immaculate tonal pitch, shows how a 19th-century artist with his grand feeling for nature could use a classical sense of design to reveal the truth and not to idealise it.

But it is often in the work of the less than very famous names that the feel of an artistic spirit and movement can be readily discerned. The work of the 18th-century Thomas Jones, such as *An Excavation* or *In The Colosseum*, shows an artist striving for the observed facts and tones of nature, and yet still somewhat clinging to the pictorial traditions to see him through. John Linnell, in his *Twickenham*, of some 35 years later, seems free from the studio props: he simply paints what he is looking at, simply but not innocently. He has invented for himself his own language. Not least fascinating were the works on view of Lord Leighton, whose off-duty landscapes have a veracity extraordinary from the hand of an artist famed in his own time for his grandly contrived figure paintings.

These Painters before Nature, both the greater and the lesser known, released for their successors perhaps more than they could know. They played no small part themselves and through their heirs, the Impressionists, the Post-Impressionists and the Fauves, in liberating painting from the picturesque.

COLIN HAYES

Some Chantrey Favourites

Love Locked Out, A Hopeless Dawn, The Last Voyage of Henry Hudson. Titles to be conjured with; titles of subjects which paradoxically reflect the Victorian social awareness that attempted to bring about lasting memorials to those qualities which had brought such prosperity to the nation.

It was that achievement and optimism which led the sculptor Sir Francis Chantrey R.A. to form a Bequest to found a national collection of British Art for which he had a deep personal concern. He bequeathed the whole of his personal estate of £105,000 after the death of his wife, for "the encouragement of British Fine Art in Painting and Sculpture only", by means of the purchase with the income of the residuary estate, "of works of Fine Art of the highest merit in painting and sculpture that can be obtained . . . by artists of any nation provided the same shall have been entirely executed within the shores of Great Britain". The purchasing income from the Bequest to be administered by the President and Council of the Royal Academy of Arts. This began in 1877 with, among others, *Athlete Wrestling with a Python* (full size bronze) by Lord Leighton P.R.A. and William Hilton's *Crown of Thorns* (oil).

This list continues with, what can only be described as, Victorian Favourites – Orchardson's *Napoleon on Board the Bellerophon* (1880), Tuke's *All Hands to the Pumps* (1889), Gotch's *Alleluia* (1896) – familiar to many as reproductions on sitting-room walls and boarding house bedrooms. As the years went on, some provocative and evocative titles stand out, such as *Lucretia Borgia reigns at the Vatican* (1914) by Frank Cadogan Cowper, *Forward the Guns!* (1917) by Lucy Kemp Welch. It is also salutary to note that the marble Roman Baths of Alma Tadema's *A Favourite Custom* (1909) was, in part, an inspiration to Cecil B. de Mille for his epic films.

There are surprises, such as Alfred Stevens's 30 cartoons and 60 designs for Dorchester House. More understandable acquisitions were *A Cotswold Farm*

(1932) by Gilbert Spencer, (brother of Stanley, relatively unknown at the time but later to become a respected Academician) and *The Jester* – a portrait of W. Somerset Maugham – by Gerald Kelly purchased in 1933. James Bateman's *Commotion in the Bullring* (1936) vies with Tissot's *The Ball on Shipboard* (1937).

It is rather difficult to assess the overall quality of the collection when one compares these with Jacob Epstein's *Mrs McEvoy* (1953); *Summer: Young September's Cornfield* by Alan Reynolds (1956), *Lytton Strachey* (1957) by Henry Lamb; *Mrs Dylan Thomas* (1955) by Anthony Devas; *Three Suffolk Towers* (1962) by John Piper.

There were further significant purchases in 1962, *The Vorticists at the Restaurant of the Tour Eiffel: Spring 1915* by William Roberts and *Mending Cowls, Cookham, 1914* by Stanley Spencer. The following year, *Ju-Jitsu 1913* by David Bomberg was bought. In a collection of this kind, tastes tend to be reflected and mistakes possibly made, as in any selection, but no one could now argue with, for example, the purchase of Stanley Spencer's *St. Francis and the Birds*, in 1967.

So it goes on; *Sheffield Weir 1954* by Edward Middleditch (1968); *Composition: Dux et Comes* by Edward Wadsworth (1969); *Beach with Bathers* by Richard Eurich (1971); in 1972, *Pink and White Turnips* by Eliot Hodgkin (whose work had already been bought by the Bequest as far back as 1936). Oddly not accepted by the Tate Gallery, which has first refusal on such purchases, was among others, David Tindle's portrait of John bought in 1974 and Ruskin Spear's *Mackerel* (1975). However, Tate acquisitions were, rightly, an early work by David Jones, *The Garden Enclosed*, and Peter Greenham's fine portrait of *Father d'Arcy* (1976); Rodney Burn's *Figures by a Lakeside* (1977); *Annociade* by John Lessore (1978); Sheila Fell's *Maryport* (1980) and this year, *L'Heure du Thé* by Anthony Green.

The Chantrey Bequest has provoked perennial controversy. Questions in the Commons, Lords, Select Committees of both Houses, Analyses, fuelled by sound art historical argument as to the validity and quality of a collection which even as the eclectic property of the Nation, could not, cannot, and probably never will, be found a home in its entirety.

The conflict of considered opinion has frustrated Chantrey's naïve benefaction. However, the list of over 600 paintings and 80 sculptures remain, in the greatest part, a catalogue of what he would have wished for his legacy.

From *Carnation, Lily, Lily, Rose* (1885–6) by J. S. Sargent to Peter Greenham's *Father d'Arcy* (1976) there is an unbroken aesthetic thread (cynics may add "bare" in places) linking the choice of paintings and, from Sir Alfred Gilbert's *Eros*

(c. 1890) to George Fullard's *Infant with Flower* (1973), linking the sculptures – drawings and wax maquettes were considered by Chantrey not to be of sufficient permanence for such a collection – a choice which must be acknowledged; were it to be made for whatever reasons, whether artistic, personal, political or purely hedonistic: a choice which may be justly challenged, on each occasion it is made, by the lofty criterion – "of the highest merit . . . (having) regard solely to the intrinsic merit of the work in question".

The collaboration, which the Academy shared with the Tate Gallery to show 45 "Chantrey Favourites" to celebrate the bicentenary of his birth, proved the wide range of the Bequest made by succeeding Presidents and Council, being rather like stonemasons working on a Gothic Cathedral, knowing that they will not see the finished work but trusting in their successors to bring it about.

The public may question, the Pundits argue, but the Nation owns the collection and the title of Grace Golden's *Free Speech* (1940) inspires the debate to continue, hopefully, into a harmony that will consummate Chantrey's Bequest.

HANS FLETCHER

William Roberts, R.A.   *The Vorticists at the Restaurant of the Tour Eiffel: Spring 1915*

Some Chantrey Favourite

John Singer Sargent, R.A.   *Carnation, Lily, Lily, Rose*

T. Jones   *In the Colosseum*

213th Summer Exhibition 1981

There is little doubt that the activity by which the Royal Academy has become best known to the public, and certainly the one which has affected most artists in the country, is its annual Summer Exhibition. First held in 1769, only four months after the institution was founded, it has taken place every year subsequently without a break in the sequence so that the latest, in 1981, was the 213th in the series.

Such an exhibition, of the work of living artists, was one of the two principal objects which the early Members had in view (the other being the establishment of the Academy's Schools of Art) and it was duly incorporated in the Instrument of Foundation signed by George III on 10 December, 1768. Rules for it were drawn up within a few weeks and in fact form the basis of the regulations still in force today. Any works which come within the categories of paintings, drawings, prints, sculptures or architectural designs and models are eligible but they must be originals (not copies) and be submitted by the artists themselves. There are no bars as to the age or nationality of participants and no qualifying limitations.

It is the Council of the Royal Academy who have the duty of selecting and hanging the exhibition and, in that they are all Members, duly elected Royal Academicians or Associates, being artists "of high attainment in their several professions", they certainly have the necessary authority and experience for the task. Moreover, as they serve on Council by rotation and thus all Members become involved from time to time, there is a wide basis of judgment which, over the years, encompasses the whole spectrum of works likely to be submitted. Their objective is to reflect what the artists of today are producing and to show it to its best advantage. They would be the first to admit that this is an almost impossible brief, particularly in that they are first of all limited to a choice from what is sent in and then to the potentiality of the galleries, but the result is always at least both catholic and debatable. In that what is superlative in art and what is less so cannot really be defined and that, by the law of averages, masterpieces cannot be expected all that often in a lifetime, artists can but strive for imaginative design and competent execution. Their contemporary audience can express praise or misgivings but ultimate judgment has to be left to posterity.

The great advantage which the Summer Exhibition brings to artists is to have their work on public display and thus have it seen, and hopefully discussed, by large numbers of people, at least some of whom will be likely purchasers. This has certainly been achieved throughout the years and there has been tremendous growth in the totals of submissions, exhibits and sales over the two centuries, also in the coverage by newspapers and periodicals and nowadays by radio and television. Whatever criticisms may have been levelled at the exhibition at various times in the Academy's history, the annual event has never passed unnoticed. There are those who have said it is too big while others have complained of its not being large enough; many have found it too crowded in its arrangement while some (particularly artists whose work has been left out) have thought it too sparsely hung; it has been censured both for being old–fashioned and for being too *avant-garde*, for being too mixed and too much of a muchness, for being held too frequently and, conversely, for not being a continuous performance, with a number of items constantly changing, through each and every year.

The first exhibition (25 April to 27 May, 1769) took place in a hired room in Pall Mall and comprised only 136 works, including paintings by Reynolds and Gainsborough. The immediately succeeding exhibitions continued there on comparable dates and quickly increased in size, extending to over 400 exhibits in 1779. No limit seems to have been set on the total submitted by individuals and Reynolds frequently showed 12 or more pictures. By the following year the Strand Block of the present Somerset House had been built and the Academy came into possession of splendid apartments there. Its exhibitions were held on the top floor (the pride of which was the Great Room, undoubtedly at that date the finest gallery in England for displaying pictures) for over 50 years, from 1780 to 1836, and the increased accommodation enabled yet more works to be displayed, the total exceeding 1,000 in 1800 and subsequent years. The number of visitors also grew considerably and the exhibition receipts from that time onwards covered the institution's expenses for many years, indeed until the first world war.

Even in these early days there were of course artists who were disappointed that their works had not been hung. Needlework and artificial flowers were apparently allowed in other exhibitions of the time but were specifically excluded from the

Academy from 1771 onwards; models in coloured wax were also not accepted. Works by Members were not (and still are not) above jurisdiction. Nathaniel Hone was made to alter the crucifix in one of his pictures lest it gave offence and this artist was in more serious trouble in 1775 when the Council refused his picture *The Conjuror*, the content of which imputed plagiarism to Reynolds and included a sketch of a nude female figure (later painted over) which Angelica Kauffman thought was meant to represent her. James Ward withdrew all his pictures in 1804 following the rejection of a very large one which he had submitted, and even John Constable had a landscape turned down. "It has been properly condemned as a daub," he said, "Send it out."

There were also artists whose work had been accepted and who then sought to influence the hanging. The most famous example was Gainsborough who, in April, 1783, wrote as follows:

"To the Council of the Royal Academy,

Mr. Gainsborough presents his compliments to the Gentlemen appointed to hang the pictures at the Royal Academy; and begs leave to hint to them, that if the Royal Family, which he has sent for this Exhibition (being smaller than three quarters) are hung above the line along with full-lengths, he never more, whilst he breaths, will send another picture to the Exhibition. This he swears by God."

The Council complied with his request but, when he wrote again on similar lines in the following year, saying:

". . . as he has painted the Picture of the Princess, in so tender a light, that notwithstanding he approves very much of the established line for strong Effects, he cannot possibly consent to have it placed higher than five feet & a half, because the likeness & Work of the Picture will not be seen any higher; therefore at a word, he will not trouble the Gentlemen against their inclination, but will beg the rest of his Pictures back again . . ."

the Council refused to be dictated to and ordered his pictures to be taken down.

There was never officially "a picture of the year" but certain works became known as such due to their great popular appeal, such as Wilkie's *Blind Man's Buff* in 1813, which had "ever a crowd round it closely packed", or Lawrence's *Calmady Children* in 1824. Other works which subsequently have become famous, such as Constable's *The Haywain* in 1821, seem to have been hardly noticed. His paintings were often severely criticised, in particular for his use of numerous touches of white and, in 1830, Turner's *Jessica* was described as "an incomprehensible daub".

As the number of artists in the country increased, but the available exhibition space at the Academy remained the same, so the competition for the inclusion of works developed. A limitation of eight submissions per artist was imposed and more works were crowded into the exhibitions at Somerset House (for example, 1,278 in 1830) but the problem has continued unresolved ever since and, indeed, has become much worse. The Academy's move to Trafalgar Square in 1837 (in part of the building subsequently completely occupied and enlarged for the National Gallery) helped a little but insufficiently and hopes were even more greatly raised when the Academy took over Burlington House, Piccadilly, in 1869 and built its exhibition galleries (and schools) on the gardens. In the first year there over 4,500 works were submitted and 1,320 of them formed the exhibition which was open to the public for three months and drew 315,000 visitors.

This is still the pattern of the Summer Exhibition as we know it today but the problems have continued to increase, particularly for the disappointed artists whose works are not included. One such published a pamphlet in 1875 and the following lines from it can hardly fail to elicit sympathy:

> The toil of months, experience of years,
> Before the dreaded Council now appears:-
> It's left their view almost as soon as in it –
> They damn them at the rate of three a minute –
> Scarce time for even faults to be detected,
> The cross is chalked:- 'tis flung aside 'REJECTED'.

The current situation is that annually some 5,000 artists submit about 12,000 works (Members being allowed six and Non-Members three each) and, from these, an exhibition of around 1,400–1,500 is formed.

The preliminary selection lasts a week and takes the form of works being passed one by one before the Council sitting in a semi-circle. True, the rate of rejection is frequently far greater than 'three a minute' by such experienced eyes but, if there is doubt, time is always spent on more intense consideration of individual works. Some 8,000 are chalked with a cross as rejected and the remaining 4,000 stay in the galleries for another two weeks during which time the Council inspect and sort them again and again in hanging and placing the final exhibition. There are works which the majority agree must be included but, inevitably, in the final analysis, others are omitted which might just as well have been chosen, and vice-versa. One thing appears to be constant in that successive Councils are somewhat despondent after their first day or so at hanging, saying that there are not sufficient good works for a really fine exhibition, and later they spend their last two or three days desperately trying to find suitable space for a few of these self-same works which they then claim, because of their merit, simply must be hung.

The attendances are always good, certainly far higher than at any other regular exhibition of contemporary art in the country, although nowadays they never exceed those of the palmy days of the late 19th century when it seems that everyone was expected to go to church each Sunday and to the Royal Academy once a year.

Frith's painting *The Private View of the Royal Academy, 1881* (shown again in this the centenary year) is evidence of the Academy as the "art establishment" of the time whereas now it is perhaps the most independent such institution. Among the innumerable "pictures of the year" during the last century, there have been *Boulter's Lock – Sunday afternoon* by E. J. Gregory (1897), *A Fallen Idol* by the Hon. John Collier (1913), *I dreamt that I dwelt in marble halls* by George Belcher (1936), *Pauline in the Yellow Dress* by James Gunn (1944) and *Her Majesty The Queen* by Pietro Annigoni (1955). This line may now be said to be continued by an award, started in 1977 (and currently financed by the British Petroleum Company Ltd.), to the artist whose work is selected as Exhibit of the Year by receiving the most votes from visitors to the exhibition, the winner this year being Robert H. Lowe for his painting *Tales of the Alhambra*; also by a prize donated by Pimm's Ltd. on similar voting by the Press, won by Carl D. Laubin for his painting *Blakeney Point*. In addition, since 1978, the President and Council, on the recommendation of a specially appointed panel, have been able to make awards through the Charles Wollaston Fund for the most distinguished work in the exhibition. This year's winner was Anthony Eyton, A.R.A. for his painting *A Fireplace* and there were runners-up prizes for *Muriel Belcher ill in bed* by Michael Clark and for a sculptured relief *Royal Academy Schools' Corridor* by Christopher J. Dean.

However meritorious these works may be, the strength of the 1981 exhibition was as usual in the great variety of the 1,447 exhibits which, in their differing ways, reflected the life and thoughts of our time. To many, one Summer Exhibition is not unlike its predecessor. Particular works stay in one's mind but the overall changes are almost imperceptible from one year to the next. Nevertheless they are there and very evident if one compares the exhibitions decade by decade. There must be development in art as in life itself or, as a previous President, Sir Thomas Monnington, said, "I do not believe that the Academy's function is to maintain a *status quo* or to further the acceptance of the acceptable . . . any development in art derives from perception free from preconception".

It does not of course mean that changes must be made merely for their own sake but that new approaches should be encouraged rather than stifled. This was the pioneering spirit of Sir Joshua Reynolds and his contemporaries in the 18th century and it could surely be claimed that it has blossomed again in the regime of the current President, Sir Hugh Casson, and his fellow Members. It can clearly be seen in the Academy's considerably increased activities and in the liveliness of the annual Summer Exhibition.

SIDNEY C. HUTCHISON

The Hanging Committee

William James *Melody Johnson*

1809

John Constable   *Lane near East Bergholt, with a man resting*

Painting from Nature

Joseph Mallord William Turner   *Quarry*   *Painting from Nature*

Ruskin Spear, C.B.E., R.A.   *Lord George-Brown below a portrait of William the Third*

Donald Hamilton Fraser, A.R.A.   *Power Station: Sand Dunes*

Carel Weight, C.B.E., R.A.   *The Walk*

Frederick Gore, R.A.   *A Field of Flowers and the Alpilles Romanilles*

Betty Swanwick, R.A.   *One amongst us*

William Scott, C.B.E., A.R.A. *Blue Still Life*

Norman Adams, R.A. *Hebridean Memories*

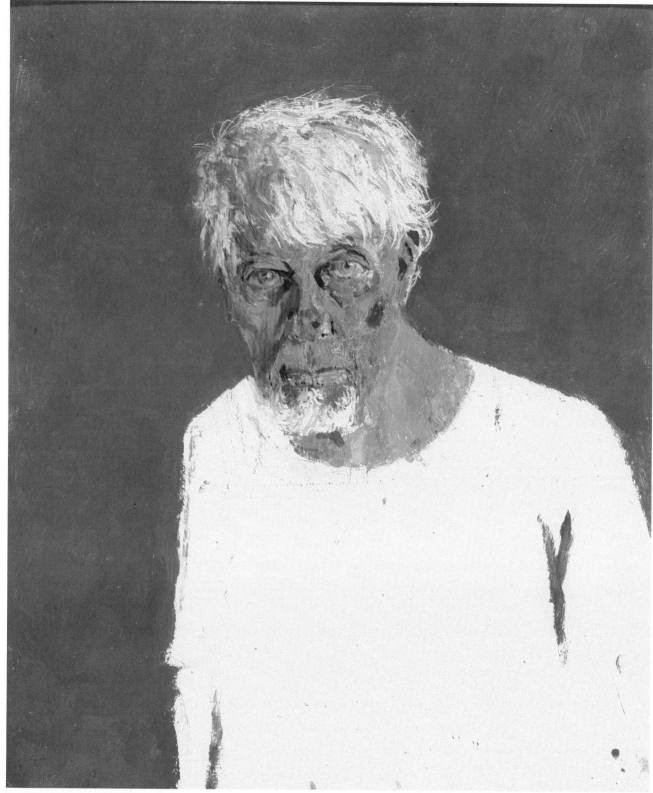

James Fitton, R.A.   *Looking at les Fauves*

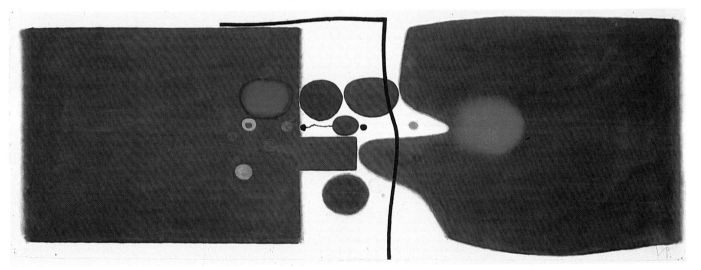

Victor Pasmore, C.H.   *A Harmony of opposing Forces, 1979–80*

Edward Bawden, C.B.E., R.A.   *Palms at Heligan*

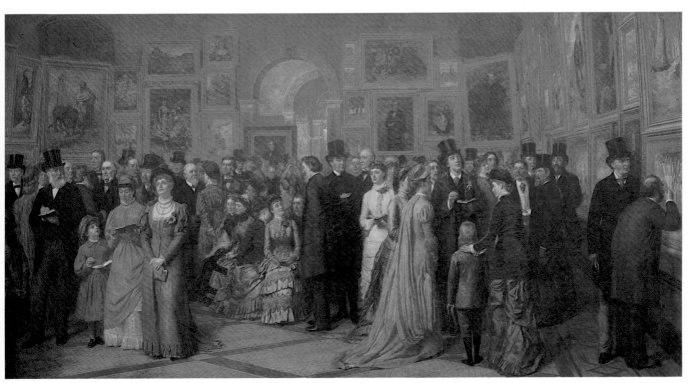

William Frith, R.A.   *The Private View at the Royal Academy, 1881*

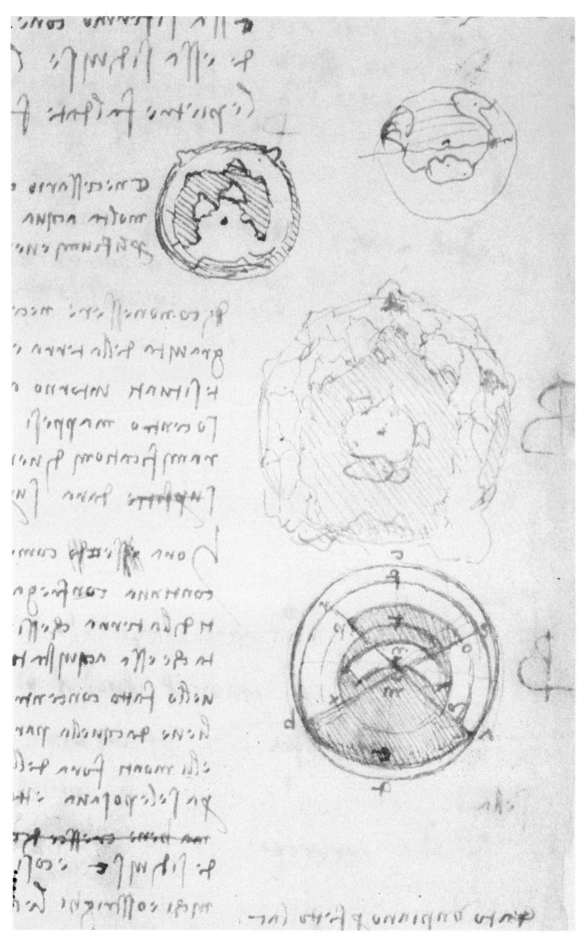

Leonardo da Vinci *Geological formation of the earth* *Codex Hammer*

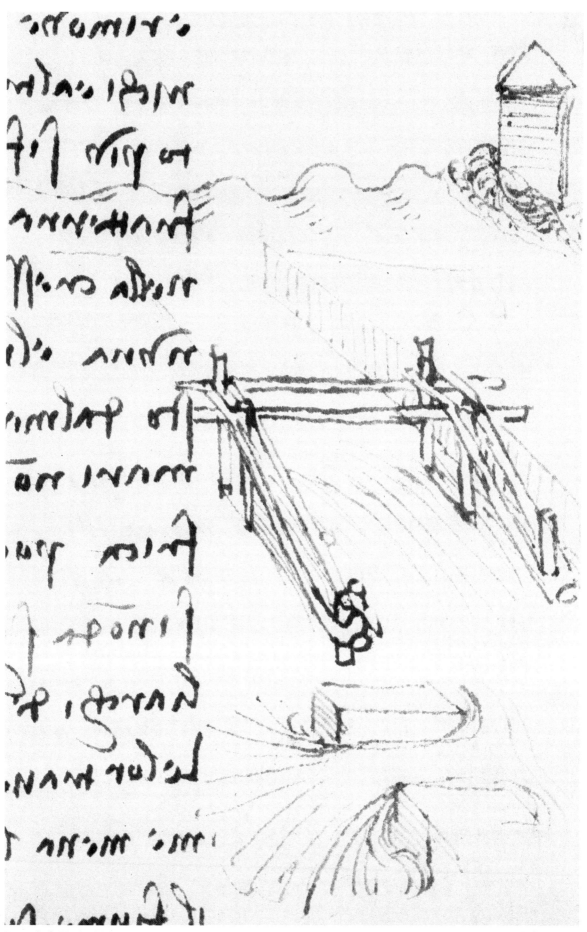

Leonardo da Vinci   *Water movement*

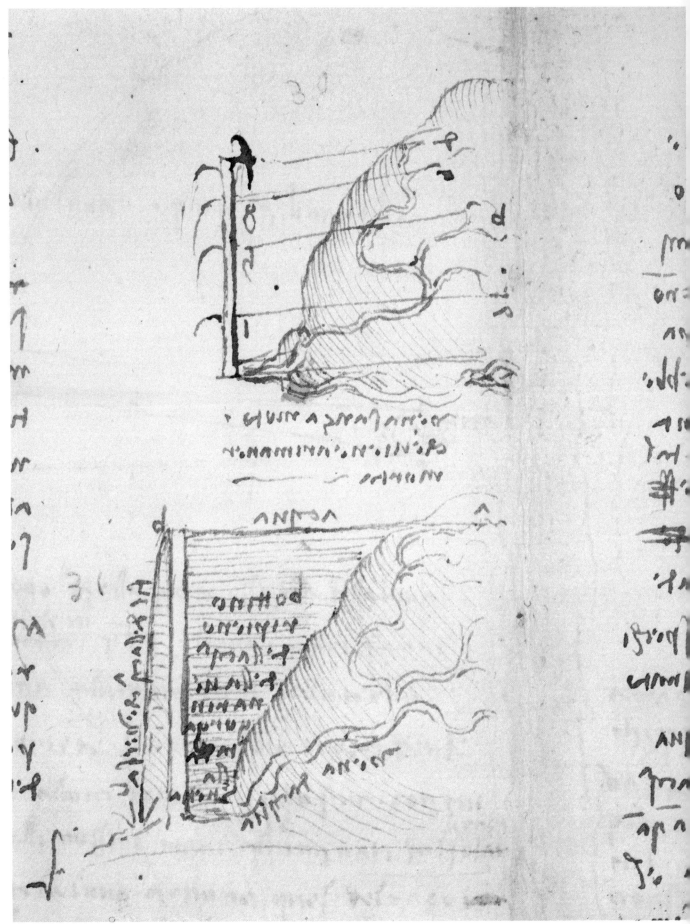

Leonardo da Vinci   *Vertical mountain section with subterranean watercourses*

Allan Gwynne-Jones, C.B.E., D.S.O., R.A.   *Poltesco Farm, Ruan Minor, Cornwall*

Peter Coker, R.A. *Agave*

B. Kneale, R.A. *Casa*

Jennifer Dickson, R.A.   *The Prisoner of Ludlow Castle*

C. Dean *Royal Academy Schools' Corridor*

Robert Buhler, R.A.   *Sydney Close*

K. Carter *John Lennon*

Jeremy Gardiner   *Komatsu*

Private View
213th Summer Exhibition

1881, a hundred years ago, was rather a special year for William Powell Frith R.A. in more ways than one. This artist, as is well known, was, *par excellence*, the master of the crowded canvas. His great set pieces, *Ramsgate Sands* (1854), *The Derby Day* (1858), *The Railway Station* (1862), *The Marriage of the Prince and Princess of Wales* (1865) and *The Salon d'Or, Homburg* (1871) stand like huge milestones down Queen Victoria's reign. Always enormous popular successes, these spectacular pictures drew ever greater crowds so that guards and railings became a familiar sight each time they were exhibited. One consequence of their popularity was that many of these pictures sired litters of replicas, to the confusion and dismay of present-day historians. Frith, however, evidently felt completely at home with crowds and replicas, to the extent of their invasion of his very life. During the two years that he was attempting to fix the crowds of Paddington on to the large canvas of his *Railway Station*, he was busy running up a replica family with a mistress, Mary Alford, who lived only a few hundred yards from the station (what an alibi!). Frith fathered altogether nineteen children – twelve by Mrs. Frith at their house a mile away and seven by Mary Alford.

His wife, Isabelle, died on 30 January 1880; a year and two days later he married Mary Alford in Paddington. Frith's powers as a painter were already on the wane when, three months later, the Private View at the Royal Academy gave him the idea for his last large composition group of modern life and, for the first time, of the world of fashion and celebrity. As usual with his more elaborate pictures it took him two years to complete.

Frith was one of those characters to whom the British have always tended to be indulgent, for he was a ceaseless scourge of pretension in art and social behaviour. Pre-Raphaelitism was a "ridiculous movement"; "the Impressionists' impressions are constant outrages on popular prejudice"; "Nocturnes" and "Symphonies" he saw as "evidence of misdirected genius". Aestheticism was, to him, no less absurd and in his *Private View* he intended "to hit the folly of listening to self-elected critics in matters of taste, whether in dress or art". Oscar Wilde, therefore, dominates to the right, while to the left stands a group of women wearing aesthetic dresses. Elsewhere in the picture are other notable figures including Gladstone, Browning, Trollope, Huxley, Leighton, Millais and Frith himself.

No one was less surprised than Frith when the picture caused a sensation at the Royal Academy in 1883, and he was doubtless gratified to see the usual railing placed before the picture with a guard to control the crowd. "I may perhaps be pardoned," he wrote "for recording the fact of this picture being the sixth painted by me that has received this special compliment." Critics, to whom Frith paid not the slightest attention, were less than complimentary. The *Magazine of Art*, for instance, found that Frith had "little to say, and says that little rather ill".

The Private View, 1881 was most felicitously hung in this year's Summer Exhibition, together with its railing. Rarely was it without its attendant crowd, and the Royal Academy in association with Christie's were offering for sale 70 photogravure prints signed by the artist. Somehow Frith still seems irrepressible.

JEREMY MAAS

Gertrude Hermes R.A.

Gertrude Hermes was elected an Associate of the Royal Academy in 1963 and an Academician in 1971. Her work has been seen regularly in Summer Exhibitions since she first showed in them in 1934. In 1981 she celebrated her 80th birthday and an exhibition covering a wide range of her work was held in the Diploma Galleries of the Academy from 12 September until 18 October 1981.

Gertrude Hermes is well known for her sculpture, wood-engravings and lino-cuts, but she has also made door-knockers and other fittings for doors, mascots for car radiators, surrounds for inn signs, a lectern for a school chapel, weather cocks in the shape of a running hare and a seahorse and a fountain at the Shakespeare Memorial Theatre at Stratford-on-Avon.

Born at Bromley, Kent, on 18 August 1901, Gertrude Hermes' first ambition was to be a farmer, and after leaving school she spent a year on a farm in Essex, milking cows and looking after pigs and hens. After studying for a year at the Beckenham School of Art, she spent four years from 1921 until 1925 at Leon Underwood's School of Painting and Sculpture at Hammersmith, drawing from the model and later starting to make sculpture, both carving in wood and modelling clay. In the 1920s and 1930s the work of Brancusi and Gaudier-Brzeska interested her greatly, as too did tribal sculpture.

Gertrude Hermes made her first wood engraving in 1922 and soon established herself as one of the leading English wood engravers of the time. A wide range of themes, including animals, plants and people, were used for prints sold individually. Illustrations were made for a number of books, published by private presses, including *The Pilgrims Progress* and *A Florilege*, as well as for the *Compleat Angler* and *The Story of my Heart* published by Penguin and selling for sixpence each. *The Garden of Caresses* was illustrated by copper engravings, the artist's only work in that medium.

In 1940 the artist's two children were invited by relatives to stay in Canada and she went with them to avoid separation. There she worked in the drawing offices of shipyards and aircraft factories making precision drawings and tracings. As a result she became 'heartily sick of black-and-white' and on her return to England in 1945 she decided to bring colour into her work, largely by making lino- and wood-cuts.

For many years Gertrude Hermes taught at art colleges both wood-engraving and lino-block cutting. In her drawing classes at the Central School in London, students were taken to the zoo to make sketches of animals, as she did herself. She is remembered with gratitude and affection by many students who gained much from her teaching.

While studying at Leon Underwood's School, Gertrude Hermes met A. P. Herbert and his wife Gwen, and Dick and Naomi Mitchison, who were to become the artist's life-long friends as well as patrons. Her first commission for a portrait in bronze was for one of A. P. Herbert in 1931. She also made busts of children, her own and those of other people Children and animals, particularly the latter, are the subjects of much of Gertrude Hermes' work. These motifs are easily sentimentalised, but never by the artist. In all her work there is marvellous balance between warmth, imagination and vitality on one side, and spareness and austerity on the other.

DAVID BROWN

Gertrude Hermes, R.A.   *Through the Windscreen*

Gertrude Hermes

The Codex Hammer

On Friday 12 December 1980, 18 large sheets of paper, bound together in red morocco and enclosed in a handsome leather box, itself disguised as a book and bearing on its upper side the gilded impression of an ostrich, were sold at Christie's for £2,200,000. In the twinkling of an eye – and one or two pairs of eyes must have been twinkling very brightly indeed – the *Codex Leicester* became the *Codex Hammer*, and simultaneously acquired a new destiny. After 263 years in England (most of them spent in the Library of Holkham Hall, Norfolk, where the genius of William Kent had provided it with a setting fully commensurate with its importance) it was now bound for California and ultimately, according to the bequest of its purchaser, Dr. Armand Hammer, a new resting-place in the Los Angeles County Museum of Art.

England will inevitably be made poorer by its departure; for most of us, however, there is little real cause to repine. Since the *Codex* is exclusively the work of an Italian, Leonardo da Vinci, we have no national claim to it apart from length of tenure, a shaky enough basis at the best of times. Its future home may not have the sumptuousness and swagger of Holkham, but will be in no way inferior where its physical well-being is concerned: even the celebrated Los Angeles smog – from which it will doubtless enjoy the most conscientious protection – could hardly be more of a potential threat than the salt-laden wind that whips across the North Sea. Most comforting of all, perhaps, is the knowledge that its sale to America will make it more, rather than less, accessible to us in this country. Between 1717 – when it was bought by Thomas Coke, later first Earl of Leicester, during his stay in Florence on the Grand Tour – and its arrival at Christie's in 1980, it was only once on public exhibition: at the Royal Academy in 1952, as part of the Leonardo Quincentenary. Even then, the fact that the originally separate folios had been bound as a book made it impossible to look at them properly. Now, on the other hand, Dr. Hammer has removed the 17th-century binding and has had each sheet separately mounted so that all can be studied together; and he has promised to make the *Codex* available in England for exhibition and study at regular intervals during and after his lifetime. The first of these exhibitions opened at Burlington House in July 1981, only seven months after the sale, and ran for 12 weeks.

So no more grumbling.

What is the *Codex Hammer*, that its fate should be a matter of such concern on both sides of the Atlantic? Essentially, it is a collection of notes and jottings by Leonardo, in his celebrated sinistral back-to-front handwriting, illustrated (usually in the margin) by diagrams and sketches. Though several of these sketches – notably a minute one of two men jumping up and down on a seesaw – are obviously by the hand of a skilled draughtsman, none of them are in any sense works of art; there is nothing, for example, remotely comparable with any of the 50 ravishing nature studies, chosen from the Leonardo collection at Windsor Castle, which made up the other half of the Royal Academy Exhibition. Why should there be? The Leonardo of the *Codex* is not the artist but the man of science – the physicist, the astronomer and, above all, the hydrologist; and he is working here not for others but for himself. Nor do the results of his labours have any particular unity, any more than most notebooks; indeed, in his lifetime, they were not a book at all. His practice, as we see it here, was simply to take a sheet, fold it down the middle to form four pages, and write till he had filled them up. The completed sheets were kept together, but had little or no direct continuity. Sometimes Leonardo even breaks off half-way down a page and starts a completely new train of thought. Only once, for a moment, does he consider the possibility of his notes being read by anyone else; on folio 2 (*verso*) he suddenly writes: "My concern now is to find cases and inventions, gathering them as they occur to me; then I shall set them in order, placing those of the same kind together; therefore you will not wonder nor will you laugh at me, Reader, if here I make such great jumps from one subject to the other."

Thus, although the *Codex Hammer* offers no particular delight to the eye, it affords us an almost unique opportunity of following the intimate thought processes of one of the greatest minds of history. Again and again, Leonardo reaches his conclusions by imagining a debate with an imaginary opponent – "*l'avversario*"; on folio 1 (*recto*) they have a fine set-to over the question of whether there are waters on the moon and what makes it shine, with Leonardo rather surprisingly upholding the water theory. (Though, after all, did not the first men on the moon land in the Sea of Tranquillity?) Later, however, he turns his attention to the phenomenon known as "the old moon in the young moon's arms" when, at the crescent phase, the whole lunar disc shows dimly luminous; and he is the first man in history to point out (correctly) that this *"lumen cinereum"* is caused by a double reflection – the sun's light being bounced back off the earth on to that part of the moon that would otherwise be in shadow. After this bull's-eye, one is a little disappointed to find him concluding that the moon is *not* responsible for tides; but then it is all too easy to forget the general state of geophysical knowledge at the beginning of the 16th century. The Pacific Ocean had not been discovered when the *Codex* was written, and the telescope was still a hundred years away in the future. What is important here is not how often Leonardo was right; it is the range and depth of his curiosity, the way the answer to one question immediately raises another in his mind, the relentless persistence with which every train of enquiry is pursued.

Of all these questions, the one which exercises him most is the movement and behaviour of water, and the ways in which it can be harnessed and controlled for man's benefit. Much of the *Codex* consists of notes for a great treatise on the subject which he planned, but never produced. There are ingenious plans for canal-building, involving locks and tunnels; schemes for the draining of marshes, the building of dams, the driving of piles into the sea bed; descriptions of the shape of a dewdrop, the way water drips from a tap, the way it moves across the surface of a bubble. There are various designs for syphons, those that will work and those that won't; diagrams illustrating the most economical or effective ways of directing a river's current; suggestions how to assess pressure or rate of flow, or how to measure the forces below the surface by observing the movement of millet seeds suspended at various depths. There are agonised discussions on whether rivers are supplied by water from the depths of the sea, drawn up through the mountains by capillary action, and endless speculations on how to explain the presence of shells or the fossils of fish on hill-tops far above sea level. Most fascinating of all, there are little sketches of the eddies and whirlpools formed when objects of various shapes and sizes are introduced into fast-flowing streams – the only drawings in the *Codex*, perhaps, that are not entirely subordinate to the written text but stand, tiny as they are, in their own right. Looking at them, I was reminded of Ruskin's description of the Rhône at Geneva: "Here was one mighty wave that was always itself, and every fluted swirl of it, constant as the wreathing of a shell. No wasting away of the fallen foam, no pause for gathering of power, no helpless ebb of discouraged recoil; but, alike through bright day and lulling night, the never-pausing plunge, and never-fading flash, and never-hushing whisper . . .'' No artist could translate such a description into visual terms as brilliantly as Leonardo, simply because no other artist understood so well *why* the water was behaving as it did; and though the *Codex* sketches are scarcely more than doodles when seen beside the majestic drawings of similar subjects in the Royal Collection, they are immediately recognisable as the seed from which the others grew.

It was a delight, at the Royal Academy, to be able to make a direct comparison between the two; but it was also inevitable that the vast majority of those who saw the exhibition – and who, like me, could not have read a word of Leonardo's diabolical script even if it had been written in the right direction – should have derived at the time infinitely more pleasure from the Windsor drawings. The *Codex Hammer* reveals little of its richness to the casual observer. The way to enjoy it is to sit down for an hour with the admirable catalogue – in which every sheet of it is fully reproduced about three-quarters actual size – and allow its author, Jane Roberts, to give one, as it were, a guided tour of its splendours. Then, and only then, does one begin to understand what an incredible treasure has been lying, forgotten except by its owners and a handful of scholars, for two and a half centuries in a Norfolk country house. And there will be any number of other surprises too: my own particular joy was the discovery, half-way down folio 8 (*recto*), of a minute drawing squashed into the margin, illustrating what must be Leonardo's least acclaimed invention. It is labelled "pea-shooter, with a hole in the middle" – "presumably", writes Miss Roberts, admirably maintaining her academic dead-pan, "so that pellets may be blown from either end simultaneously".

What a relief to know that he was human after all.

JOHN JULIUS NORWICH

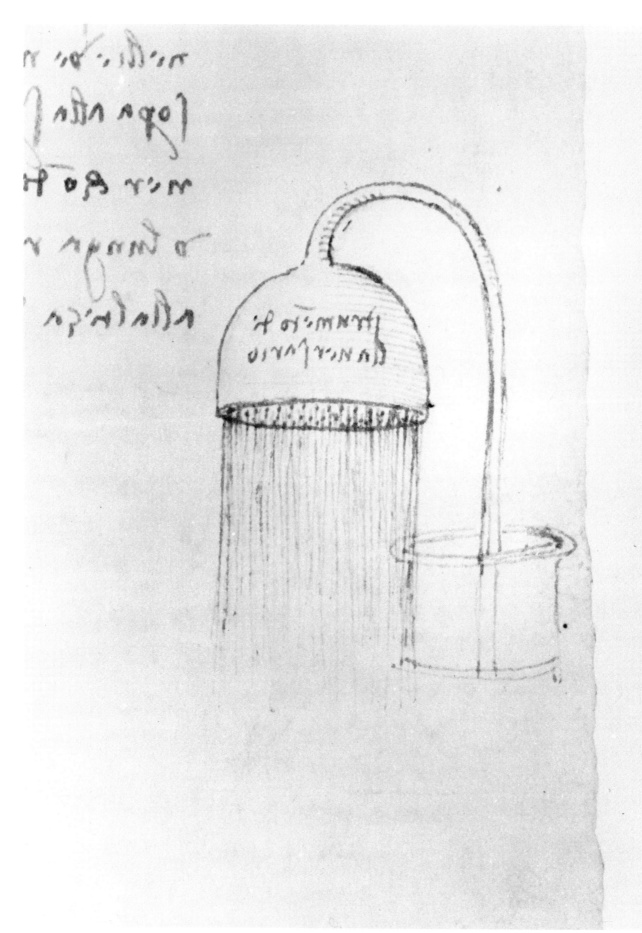

Leonardo da Vinci   *Syphon devised by an adversary of Leonardo*

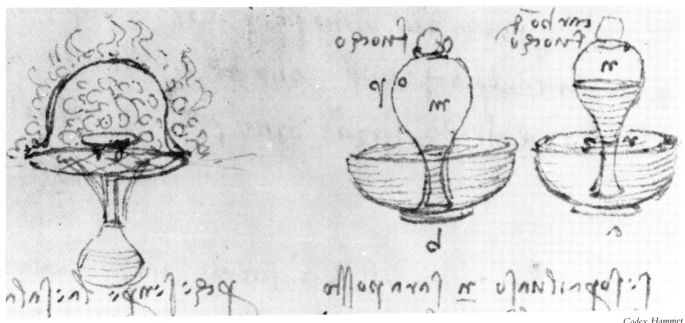

Leonardo da Vinci   *Experiments with a vacuum*   *Codex Hammer*

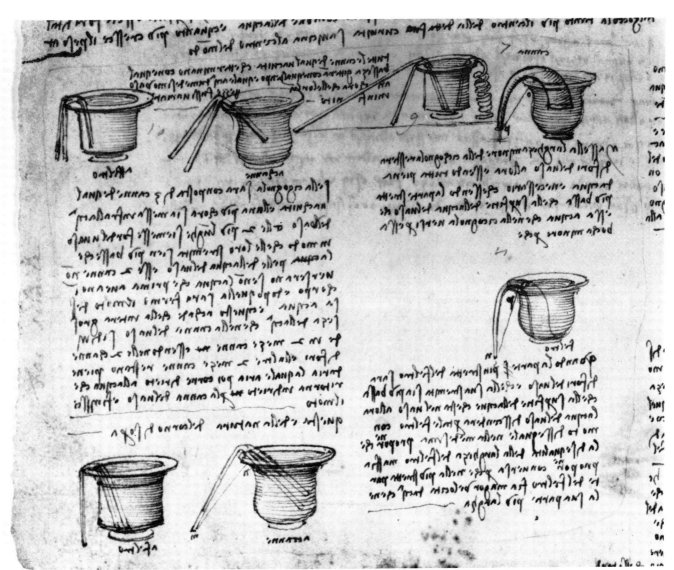

Leonardo da Vinci   *Experiments with syphons*   *Codex Hammer*

The Great Japan Exhibition

At about the time this first issue of the Royal Academy's Yearbook reaches the bookstalls, The Great Japan Exhibition, the greatest exhibition of Japanese art ever held in Europe and one of the most ambitious to be mounted by the Royal Academy, will have opened to the public, preceded, if all goes according to plan, by a veritable fanfare of publicity calculated to excite the interest of millions in this country and abroad.

This is not the place or the time for a detailed review of the contents of the exhibition, much less of the public response to it, both of which will be fully reported on in the Yearbook next year; but it does seem fitting to say something here about the concept behind the exhibition and the work of planning and organisation on which hundreds or even thousands of man-hours have been expended in both London and Japan during the 12-month period covered by this Review. That it was time for the mounting of a major exhibition of Japanese art in London had been for some years in the minds of several people interested in promoting Anglo-Japanese understanding, but the idea began to take shape in the spring of 1976 when the proposal for an exhibition concerning itself with the art and society of the Edo period was put forward by Professor William Watson. He had for some time been discussing such a project with his colleagues, Mr. Lawrence Smith, Keeper of the Department of Oriental Antiquities at the British Museum, and Dr. Oliver Impey, Assistant Keeper, Eastern Art at the Ashmolean Museum, Oxford. Their shared enthusiasm for the project stemmed from two considerations; first that it was during the Edo period (1600–1868), when Japan was for much of the time all but closed to contact with the rest of the world, that the complex, rich and very special culture developed which so greatly determined the shape of modern Japan and which continues to influence Japanese life even today; and secondly that an exhibition such as they envisaged had never before been attempted either in the West or in Japan itself.

From the first, the idea of an exhibition of the Art of Japan at the Royal Academy received encouraging support from the Japanese Embassy and from the London representatives of the Japan Foundation, a semi-governmental organisation dedicated to the promotion of mutual understanding and friendship between the peoples of the world by means of cultural exchange. But there were many obstacles to be faced by the proponents of the project, most daunting of which was finance, since it was apparent from the beginning that the cost of mounting an exhibition of Japanese art of the quality and on the scale envisaged would be huge – certainly far beyond the current resources of the Royal Academy. It was also agreed by all concerned that it would be inappropriate to make a formal approach to the Japanese side for the loan of their jealously-preserved art treasures unless there was assurance that substantial funds towards the cost would be forthcoming from British sources. Most fortunately, it was at this point that the Midland Bank came forward with an offer to act as prime sponsor to the exhibition and it was under the leadership of Midland Bank International that a group of leading British companies with strong Japanese business links was eventually brought together to assume the main financial burden and risk. The generous co-sponsors are: The *Observer*, a foremost newspaper group, Overseas Containers Ltd., a leading company in the world of shipping, Pringle of Scotland, one of the world's most prestigious manufacturers of fine cashmere garments, Shell Sekiyu K.K., the oil company who last year celebrated 80 years' presence in Japan, and the Swire Group, a major Far East Trading House. The spokesman for Midland Bank International has explained that it was in recognition of the importance of Japan to Britain that the Bank had chosen the Great Japan Exhibition as its first important sponsorship in order to contribute towards the breaking down of cultural barriers and the strengthening of the historical ties existing between the two countries.

With financial support assured, the academic advisers, who had already formulated an outline plan and drawn up agreed lists of works of art that they would wish to borrow, began working closely with their Japanese opposite numbers in the Japanese Government's Agency for Cultural Affairs (Bunka-chō). The first requirement was to sell the idea of an Edo exhibition to the Japanese scholars; a delicate task calling for the exercise of much tact, because, as already explained, the concept of an exhibition designed to show the evolution of art and society during the Edo period was, if not exactly revolutionary, certainly quite novel to Japan. It was imperative that the British side should succeed in taking their

Japanese counterparts along with them because only with their enthusiastic help would it be possible to secure the loan of the hoped-for exhibits of the greatest artistic merit, many of them scheduled in Japan as works of exceptional national importance. This was a very complicated process which required several vists to Japan by both Mr. Smith and Dr. Impey because of the large number of loans to be drawn not only from public collections and the Imperial Collection but from numerous private owners as well as from temples and shrines all over Japan. The response from the officials of the Bunka-chō can only be described as magnificent. They devoted hours of constructive work in protracted negotiations with owners and it is truly as a consequence of their unstinted efforts over the past year that the exhibition, consisting as it does of a total of some 750 works of art achieved its final form.

There were, of course, disappointments on the way. Sometimes the loan of a choice painting or other work proved not to be feasible because of technical or legal obstacles; sometimes a half-promised loan fell through unexpectedly for no clearly understandable reason. But there were also unexpected compensations as for example when it became possible to borrow such important works as the famous Ōkyo screens of Pines in the Snow and Wistaria in blossom, the painted doors of the Tenkyū in the water-wheel screens of the Tokyo National Museum and Kōrin's Peacocks and Hollyhocks. Throughout the whole process the negotiators of the Bunka-chō pursued their goal with patience and determination and it cannot be stressed too strongly how much the successful outcome of the negotiations owes to their persistence.

While these negotiations were going on, plans for the layout of the exhibits and the re-designing of the Royal Academy galleries to house them were being worked out between Kisho Kurokawa, one of Japan's foremost architects, who had been selected by the Japan Foundation as chief designer of the exhibition in partnership with Kiyoshi Awazu, and Alan Irvine the well-known British exhibition designer.

The designers decided to go for a clean ultra-modern interior avoiding the "picturesque" aspects of Japan and anything smacking of *japonaiserie*, the aim being to create a low-key or even mysterious background against which the brilliance of the exhibits would be seen to greatest advantage.

The total effect should be stunning.

The diversity and high quality of the exhibits themselves will no doubt come as a surprise to visitors to the Royal Academy this autumn, many of whom will be unaware of the richness of Japanese society during the Edo period. For example, few people in this country will know that Edo in the 17th and 18th centuries grew into the greatest stronghold and most important city in Japan and that by 1700 it had a population of more than three quarters of a million, which implies that it was one of the biggest cities in the world at that time. By 1800 the population is said to have exceeded a million. The state of peace which was preserved under the Tokugawa régime naturally encouraged economic development, and this, together with other factors, led to a great increase in the wealth and influence of the townspeople which was gained mainly at the expense of the formerly powerful samurai classes. The feudal lords and their retainers spent their money on luxury goods produced by the artisans and sold by the merchants, so by about the beginning of the 18th century most of their wealth had passed into the hands of the townspeople. This helped to bring the commoners to a position of real importance and enabled the more fortunate among them to indulge their tastes by leading a leisurely life, buying luxury goods, patronising artists and acquiring works of art, and in general enjoying that fuller life that in past times had been the prerogative of the aristocrats and the military rulers.

It is a special aim of the exhibition to show the brilliant decorative art of Edo in worthy terms, for it is no less important than painting as interpreting the Japanese taste which has had world-wide influence since the 19th century. Prints, ceramics, metalwork, items of costume and armour, weapons, lacquerware and, above all, the magnificent silk textiles which have never before been shown in such richness in the West and which form such a striking element of The Great Japan Exhibition, are the products of this remarkable society which the Royal Academy jointly with the Japan Foundation is introducing to the public this autumn.

JOHN FIGGESS

Nin'ami Dōhachi   *Tea bowl with design of a crane*   *Great Japan exhibition*

S. Ōkyo sha (copied by Ōkyo) *Pair of stirrups*

Great Japan exhibition

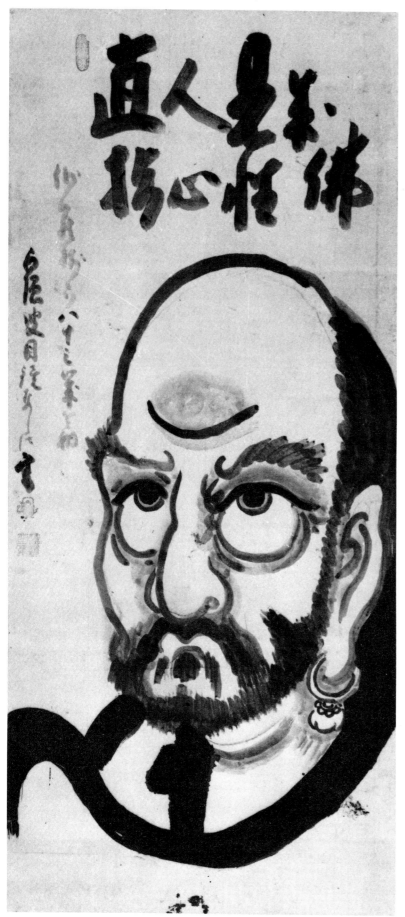

Bodhidarma in meditation

Portrait of Toyotomi Hidehoshi   *Great Japan exhibition*

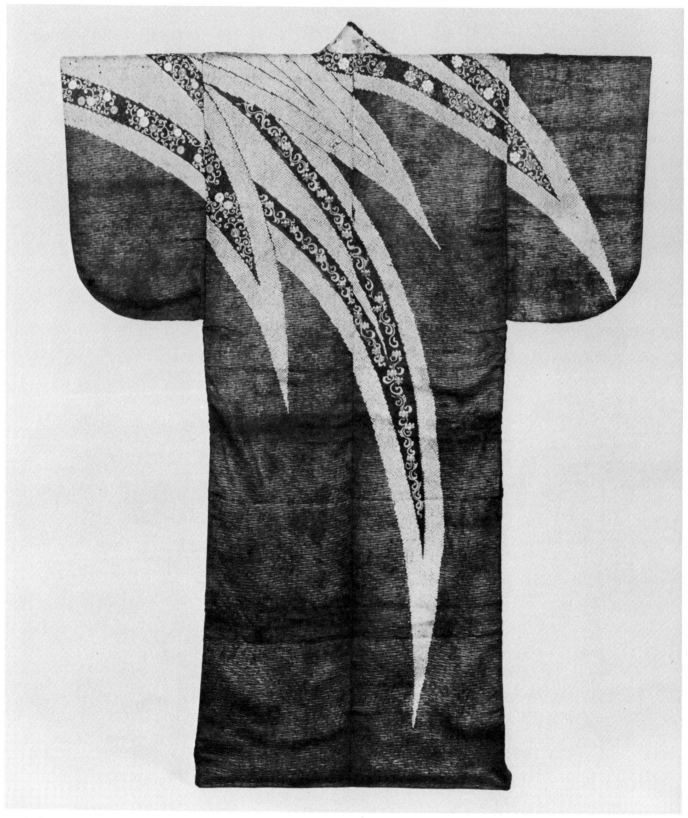

Kosode of purple silk in huihaku with grass-blade pattern

Royal Academy Schools Finals

The Royal Academy Schools, which have now been in existence for over 200 years, are tucked away at the back of Burlington House, in what might look like the servants' quarters of this resplendent palace of art (or a more appropriate contemporary analogy might be, the Communications and Intelligence Rooms of a presidential palace); but let it not be forgotten that they were the prime reason for the founding of the Royal Academy. Until only a few years ago and the Academy's financial straits, they maintained the original commitment to free tuition – which means that around 7,000 artists have passed through the Schools as students by now, almost all for free; famous, less famous, practitioners and teachers.

The first students at the Schools, when Burlington House was extended to form the Royal Academy premises in 1868, would still be able to find their way around the Schools blindfold – little has changed: businesslike studios with a steady northern light, modest facilities, and corridors punctuated with casts of great classical sculpture – corridors whose human traffic is quieter than in most educational institutions, since in term time there will be several easels set up in front of the casts.

For the other chief aspect of the Schools that has not changed is the emphasis on (lively) drawing from life; indeed, for the first term of the three years of their time in the Schools, new students spend the whole time in life drawing. It is an amusing tribute to the Schools' steady devotion to providing this basic training, and teaching art rather than fashions in art, that 'drawing what you see' and drawing from the living model – which were standard practice when the Academy was created, but which practically disappeared from art-schools during the 1960s and early 1970s (making the Academy Schools the refuge of students who wanted to do just this) – are back in fashion again in the art world at large. However, the Academy's facilities for working from a live model are still exceptional; and this naturally draws to the Schools, students who are interested in learning from nature, before embarking on their individual careers as artists.

The Academy Schools offer three full-time courses, all of three years, each geared to various qualifications and needs: for those with no previous art-school training except a year's foundation course; those who come equipped with a previous three years' training, but from an art college not qualified to award degree status; and those who already have a degree from an art college or a university. However, talent, application and artistry being what they are, it is not always easily discernible, in the final exhibition of the students' work in June of their third year, just which students have been on which course.

This annual exhibition of about 500 works by about 30 "passing-out" students, a third of the Schools' total complement of around 90, has its own particular flavour. Each year, granted, has a particular character of its own (the students support each other's work more, probably, in these smaller schools); but where, in other art schools' degree shows, the emphasis is more often on individuality and there is a sense of being hopefully well on the way to professional art-gallery showing, at the Academy there is the sense that these are still students, and happy to be, preparing slowly and thoroughly for a lifetime's career of further discovery; and keeping close to subjects "from life": that neglected tradition which David Hockney recently described as "expressing what it was they were looking at – what it was about it that delighted them – and how that delight forced them to make something of it, to share the experience, to make it vivid to somebody else". The extension of this human impulse to the most professional and subtle levels of experience and art is surely what the Academy, and the Academy Schools, are about.

It was an attractive "Finals" exhibition this year. One pleasing feature was that the three strong sculptors, Lonsdale, Kobayashi and Zuvac, had arranged the sculpture studios as an integrated three-man show, rather than the all-too-familiar "private box" arrangement. Among the painters – whose work ranged as usual from the modest to the expressionist and the real to the surreal – I must single out Grahame Hurd-Wood, for just that sharing of visual delight that Hockney talks of and which the Academy Schools aim to give depth to; on the other hand, Kitty Reford's work reminds us that what art students are seeking is the whole technique – skill, strength, power, discipline and freedom and art to be, ultimately, themselves. And Graham Jones' work is another reminder from the very centre of "academic" studies: that the visual thrills of the present moment meet minds which are heir to nearly 3,000 years of high civilisation and high art, and that the meeting of the two can be profound.

Art schools are *always*, by their nature, in a delicate balance between this rich tilth and present needs; and between the individual and the universal; and the Academy Schools are at the very heart of this immensely important (and sometimes one feels, thankless) task.

MICHAEL SHEPHERD

Timothy Crocker   *Sugar Beet Lifter*

R.A. Schools – Installation, 1981

Rowlandson   *R.A. School*

Arrival of a Portuguese ship at Nagasaki, with a Jesuit chapel

Flowering plum with pheasants

Ogata Kōrin *Writing box with design of Ariwara nō Narihira on a fan* *Great Japan exhibition*

Katabira of indigo hemp, tie dyed and embroidered

Early European Visitors Arriving in Japan (Pair of six-fold screens. Colour on gold-leafed paper)

Maruyama Ōkyo *Pines in the snow* *Great Japan exhibition*

Leonardo da Vinci   *The 'Pointing Lady'*

Leonardo da Vinci   *Branch of Blackberry*

Nature Studies

Leonardo da Vinci   *A 'Star of Bethlehem' and other plants*

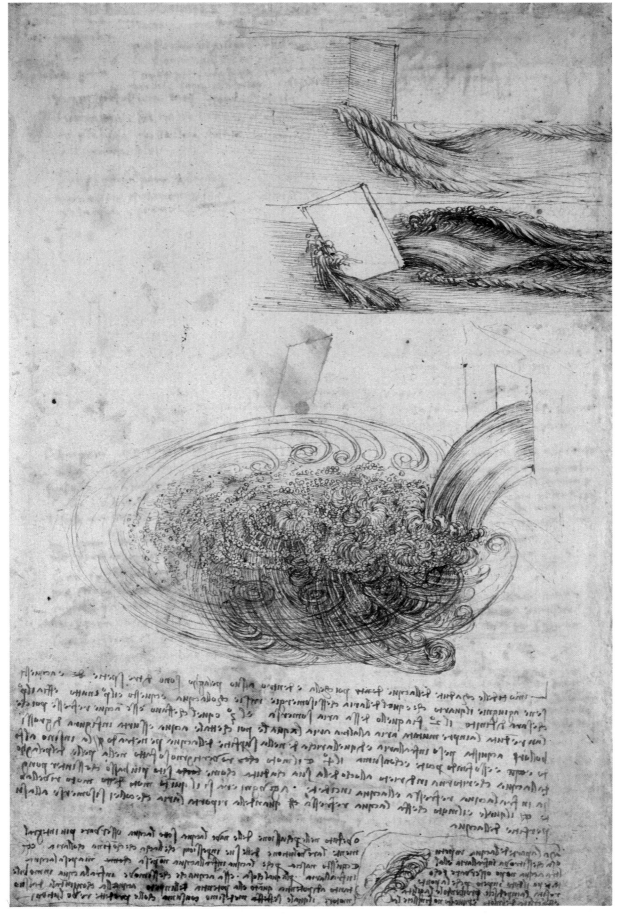

Leonardo da Vinci   *Sheet of studies of water passing obstacles and falling into a pool, with notes*

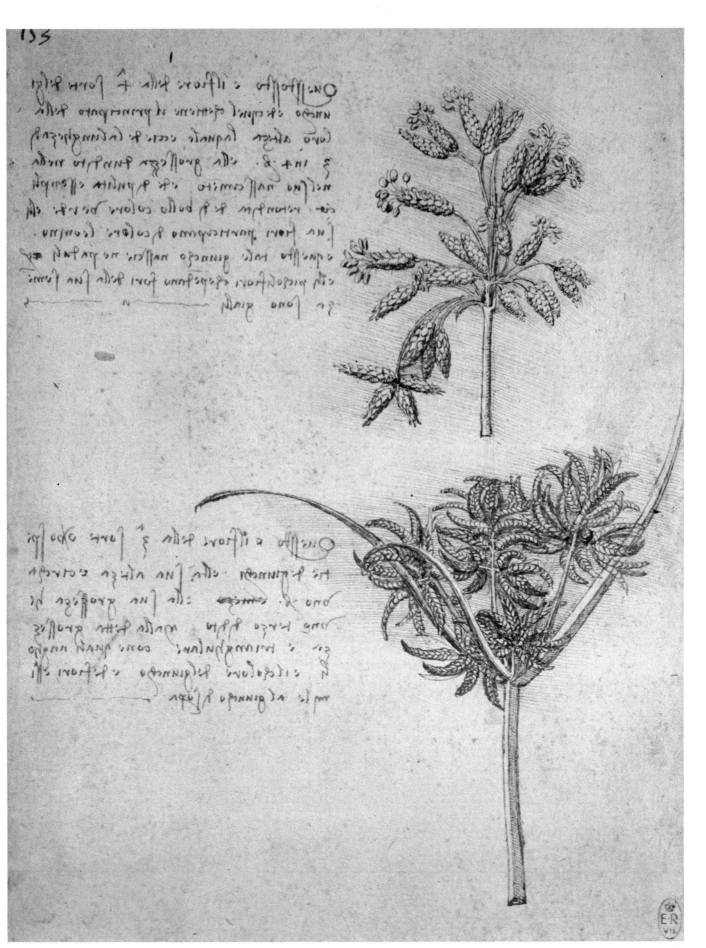

Leonardo da Vinci   *Houses above a canal running by a winding river*   *Nature Studies*

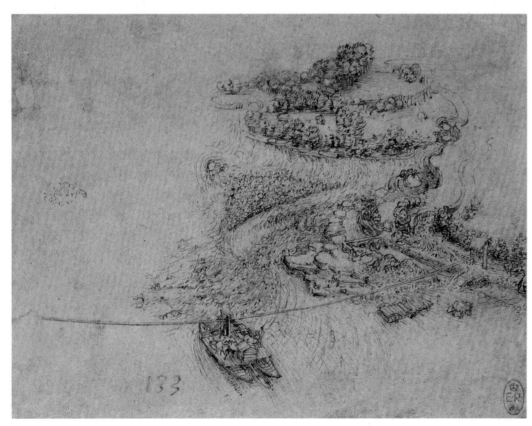

Leonardo da Vinci   *Bird's-eye view of a ferry swinging across a river*   *Nature Studies*

The Nature Studies of Leonardo Da Vinci

Those few but majestic Alpine peaks which exceed the magic height of 4,000 metres are known with reverence as "*Viertausender*". The artistic giants of the High Renaissance need some more subtle criterion than one of quantity to distinguish them from their lesser brethren. If output of finished works of art, for example, were an important factor, the name of Leonardo da Vinci might well not be found among them, as his was slender compared with that of rivals such as Michelangelo and Raphael. His pictures may be superb, but they were always few, and some have not survived. The two great works of sculpture on which he spent so much thought and labour were never completed, and all physical trace of them has perished. Is his reputation then largely based on the judgement of his contemporaries? By no means, towering though his stature was during his lifetime. Today the imprint of his genius is apparent most directly in his surviving drawings (including his scientific diagrams), and these are numerous.

Drawings are less spectacular than most other forms of art. Always small, often lacking in colour, they have little or no part to play in the embellishment of great houses, and so lack the prestige that goes with wealth and rank. In earlier centuries no one in his senses would have collected them unless they really meant something to him. But to the discerning eye they have more to say than many a highly worked painting or sculpture. Sometimes they record an artist's first thoughts in shaping a composition, mediating between inner idea and final outer representation. Others may serve as a kind of visual notebook, giving form to concepts or configurations that would take an age to describe in the cumbersome mechanism of words. Leonardo knew the dangers of excessive reliance on prose. "Do not busy yourself," he urges "with things belonging to the eyes by making them enter through the ears." To give a close insight into the genius of such a man no medium could be better fitted than that of drawing.

And Leonardo is the very archetype of genius. Lacking a formal education, he had little respect for established authorities in any field of study, but made Nature his instructor. When, for example, he wanted to discover what the human body was made of, and how it worked, he secured a succession of cadavers, took a knife, and looked for himself, making a visual and verbal record of what he saw. His anatomical drawings are not only a miracle of draughtsmanship, performing their descriptive function with a clarity which put contemporary anatomists to shame: they are also immeasurably more accurate than their textbook equivalents of his day, justifying his contempt for traditional learning, whose main effect, insofar as he could not escape its influence, was to lead him astray.

So it was in the many other areas to which Leonardo directed his insatiable quest for knowledge, and there were few fields of inquiry about the natural world on which he did not turn his gaze. This was no idle curiosity. His close understanding of the principles of what we now call mechanics, for example, made him one of the most sought after military engineers of his day. And in his refusal to entertain as fact any statement not derived from objective investigation he ranks among the founding fathers of modern science. When he died at Amboise in 1519 the record of his incessant researches was to be found on several thousand sheets of paper in his studio, sometimes in the form of drawings, sometimes as verbal commentary inscribed in his idiosyncratic writing, which ran from right to left like Arabic. Despite substantial losses over the centuries more than enough has survived to establish the breadth of his interests, the accuracy of his observation, and the extraordinary fertility of his invention.

The largest surviving collection of these drawings is now in the Biblioteca Ambrosiana at Milan. This contains more than 2,000 folios, chiefly concerned with engineering and allied subjects. Second in size but far more interesting in content is a collection of 600 folios which migrated to England by way of Spain in the first half of the 17th century, and at an unknown time before its close came into possession of the British Crown. Which monarch had the knowledge and good fortune to secure this prize is uncertain. Some evidence points towards King Charles I, who was not only one of the greatest collectors of paintings of all time, but certainly included drawings in his collection. Other indications suggest King Charles II. Be that as it may, they were seen in Kensington Palace in 1690, when William and Mary were on the throne, and have belonged to the sovereigns of this country ever since.

This collection comprises almost all the surviving drawings by Leonardo on what may be broadly described as artistic subjects, including studies for his paintings and sculptures. In addition it contains all but one of his surviving anatomical drawings. When it came into royal hands it was housed in a single volume, into which all the drawings had been bound by an earlier owner. Drawings so mounted cannot of course be separately exhibited, and the very act of turning the pages in order to look at them places them at risk, especially where, as in Leonardo's later work, they are executed wholly or partly in chalk. During the last century they were liberated from this binding, and many were placed in separate sunk mounts, which gave them better protection for handling and exhibition. Folios bearing drawings on both sides of the paper could not of course be treated in this way: and it is only recently that a satisfactory method of mounting them has been devised. This consists of a thin sandwich formed by two panes of transparent plastic sheeting, enclosing the two-sided drawing in the middle, all placed within a thick cardboard mount furnished with an opening on either side. Even drawings whose versos are blank are now being mounted in this way, so as to ensure complete protection for the fabric of the paper, while leaving the verso open to view in case any markings on it may subsequently be found to have significance.

This method of mounting was first applied to the anatomical series, and made their exhibition at the Royal Academy possible in 1977. It was then extended to a category loosely described as landscapes, plants and water studies, which formed the content of this year's exhibition. Other categories remaining to be so treated consist of horses and other animals, figure studies, caricatures and allegories and a miscellaneous section which includes architecture, science, technology and maps.

The series of landscapes and other nature studies from which this year's exhibition was chosen exemplifies at its deepest level the fusion in Leonardo's mind of the attitudes of artist and scientist, attitudes which tend in lesser beings to be mutually exclusive. This impression is at its most striking in the delicate and meticulous studies of plants, intended as raw material for the foreground of oil paintings, but each a model of objective observation. His feeling for the solidity and grandeur of mountains is in no way diminished by his close understanding of geological formation; and when he observes the motion of water past obstacles with the eye of an engineer, the delicate tracery of his penwork resembles the movement of human hair, a comparison to which he himself draws attention in his detailed notes.

This does not mean that his vision is always constrained within the limits of the real. Sometimes he allows it to cross the frontier of allegory, perhaps to convey to the initiated concepts whose overt expression at the time would have been unacceptable. Sometimes, as in the famous deluge series, which depicts cosmic cataclysm, he gives his prophetic insight free rein. But however much the grand design may represent a product of the imagination, its component parts still reflect his primary allegiance to physical reality.

By a happy coincidence these drawings became available for display in London soon after the purchase by Dr Armand Hammer of a manuscript by Leonardo then known as the *Codex Leicester*. This manuscript is mainly devoted to observations on the movement of water, with their practical application in engineering, and consists of a written text illustrated by diagrams. The pages of this codex, like those of the Windsor series when they originally entered the Royal Collection, were bound into a single volume. One of Dr. Hammer's first actions on acquiring it was to separate its component leaves and have them placed on individual mounts of the same kind as those devised for the Windsor drawings. This made it possible to exhibit the two series together. Their juxtaposition has not only resulted in a much more interesting exhibition, but has also given rise, as can be seen from the scholarly catalogue of the *Codex Hammer* by Jane Roberts, to important new insights into Leonardo's ideas and work.

As the new method of mounting is extended to the remaining categories in the Windsor series, so they in their turn will become available for exhibition. The process of remounting also brings other advantages. When each drawing has been detached from its old mount and before it is inserted in the new, it is chemically stabilised (to prevent the gradual discoloration and disintegration arising from the presence of acid) and otherwise restored. The opportunity is then taken to place it directly before a colour-separation camera, the photographs from which are used for making a facsimile reproduction of the highest quality. These facsimiles, printed by the Curwen Press, are being published by the Johnson Reprint Company, a subsidiary of Harcourt Brace Jovanovich, in a series of limited editions of which the first, comprising the anatomical drawings, appeared in 1978. The next edition, which will include the landscapes and other nature studies, is due to appear in 1982. Each set of facsimiles is accompanied by a comprehensive catalogue.

Meanwhile exhibitions of those drawings which have already been remounted are sent, by gracious permission of Her Majesty The Queen, all over the world, wherever there are art-galleries or museums which possess facilities for adequate climatic and security control. The landscapes exhibition has been shewn in

California and New York, and will shortly go to Houston and Milan. The travels of the anatomical drawings have been no less extensive, and they are due in Australia in 1982. The Royal Academy's Leonardo exhibition of 1981 thus forms part of a continuing series, which started with the exhibition of the anatomical drawings at the Academy in 1977.

It is fitting that this series of exhibitions should have originated in the Academy, which has often since its foundation in the 18th century under the active patronage of King George III been regarded for the purpose of exhibitions as an extension of the royal residences. The greatest royal exhibition which its walls have witnessed occurred a few years after the second world war, when the principal oil paintings in the Royal Collection had emerged from their war-time seclusion in a Welsh salt-mine. The exhibition of the King's Pictures in 1946 was a unique event in the history both of the Royal Collection and of the Academy. "A beautiful exhibition," wrote Queen Mary in her catalogue. Six years later the Academy's exhibition to celebrate the quincentenary of Leonardo's birth included a massive loan from Windsor Castle. The creation of The Queen's Gallery at Buckingham Palace, which was opened in 1963, has provided a more regular outlet for exhibitions of works of art in the Royal Collection; indeed one devoted to Leonardo was held there in 1969. But there are other demands on the Gallery's space, and it has been a happy solution to revive the older tradition for two recent exhibitions of Leonardo's work.

ROBIN MACKWORTH-YOUNG

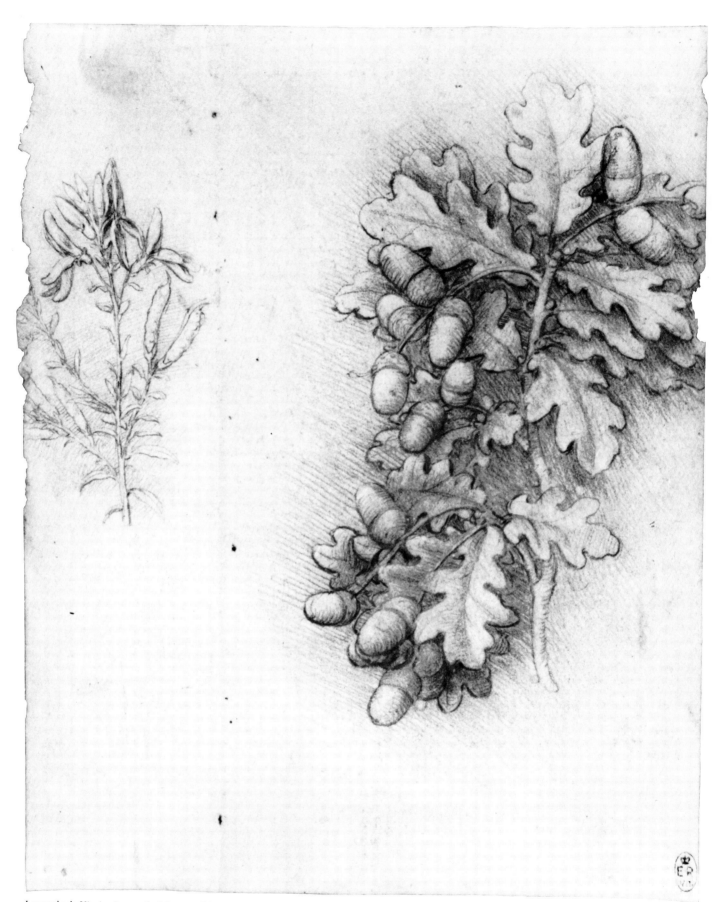

Leonardo da Vinci   *Sprays of oak leaves and Dyer's greenweed*

Leonardo da Vinci   *An old man in profile to right, seated on a rocky ledge ; water studies and a note*   *Nature Studies*

Leonardo da Vinci   *Deluge over falling trees*   *Nature Studies*

Leonardo da Vinci   *Mountain peaks, foothills and river in foreground*

Programme of Exhibitions 1982

The Great Japan Exhibition	24 Oct–21 Feb 1982
Carel Weight R.A.	9 Jan–14 Feb
Harold Gilman	25 Feb–4 Apr
Stowells' Trophy	15 Mar–21 Mar
Burlington House Fair	12 Mar–21 Mar
214th Summer Exhibition	15 May–8 Aug
Association of Consultant Architects	14 June–4 July
Elizabeth Blackadder R.A.	July–August
Modern Indian Art	September–October
William Roberts R.A.	October–December

Other exhibitions may be arranged and although every effort will be made to adhere to the basic programme and outline, the Royal Academy must reserve the right to change it if necessary. Any such alterations will be announced as far in advance as possible.

Acknowledgements

The Royal Academy and the publisher would like to thank the owners and photographers for their kindness in allowing us to use their transparencies, with special thanks to:
His Grace, The Duke of Devonshire – Treasures from Chatsworth
The Armand Hammer Foundation – Honoré Daumier, The Codex Hammer
The Arts Council – Painting from Nature
The Stanley Spencer Gallery, The National Trust and the Trustees of the Tate Gallery – Stanley Spencer, R.A.
The Tate Gallery – The Chantrey Bequest, Howard Hodgkin
The British Museum, The Ashmolean Museum and the Japan Foundation – The Great Japan Exhibition and
By Gracious Permission of Her Majesty the Queen – Leonardo da Vinci Nature Studies

The Royal Academy

The Upstairs Gallery

The Upstairs Gallery in the Royal Academy invites Friends to visit its exhibitions which are open between 10 a.m. and 6 p.m. on Tuesday to Friday, between 11 a.m. and 5 p.m. on Saturday or on Monday by appointment.

Business Art Galleries

Business Art Galleries at the Royal Academy offers special assistance to companies interested to purchase, hire or commission pictures. Further information may be obtained from Business Art Galleries, tel: 01-734 1448.

Christmas Cards and Gifts

The Royal Academy has produced a new range of Christmas cards and gifts ideally suited to people of all ages and interests. Friends are invited to view the various items in the Royal Academy Shop or study the leaflets which they have been sent. Proceeds from sales will support the exhibitions and activities of the Royal Academy.

Christmas Gift Subscriptions

Membership of the association of Friends of the Royal Academy would make a perfect Christmas gift. The annual subscription is £15.50, and there are reduced subscriptions of £12.50 for full-time teachers and museum staff, and of £10 for pensioners and young Friends under the age of 25. The Friends' Office at the Royal Academy will enclose a personal Christmas message to each new Friend on request.

Friends' Tours 1982

Friends are warmly invited to join the tours to Barcelona, Classical Greece, Japan, Lake Geneva, Cumbria, New England and Siena which have been specially arranged by the organisers of Specialtours. A brochure and further information is available from Specialtours, 2 Chester Row, London SW1W 9JH (tel: 01-730 2297) and from The Secretary, The Friends of the Royal Academy (tel: 01-734 9052).

Library

The Library of the Royal Academy is primarily intended for use by its Members, Friends and Students. Exhibitors and persons engaged in research are welcome to use it on application to the Secretary or Librarian.

The Artists' General Benevolent Institution

Patron: Her Majesty The Queen

President: Sir Hugh Casson, K.C.V.O., P.R.A.

For 167 years the A.G.B.I. has provided assistance to professional artists and their dependants in times of need. FUNDS are urgently needed for the continuation of this work. Please send subscriptions to:

The Secretary, Artists' General Benevolent Institution, Burlington House, Piccadilly, London w1v 0dj

The Royal Academy Schools

Keeper: Peter Greenham, C.B.E., R.A.

Master of the Sculpture School: Willi Soukop, R.A.

Master of Carving: A. J. J. Ayres, F.R.B.S.

Curator: Walter Woodington, R.B.A., R.P.

Secretary: Laura Scott

The Royal Academy Schools provide training in Drawing, Painting and Sculpture for students of approved ability and promise whose aim is to become practising artists.

The 7,000 former students include many of the best-known British Artists from Blake, Constable and Turner to those of the present day.

In addition to the permanent staff, a number of leading artists, both Members of the Royal Academy and others, act as visiting teachers in the Schools.

For further details, with conditions for admission, application should be made to the Curator, Royal Academy Schools, Burlington House, Piccadilly, London w1v 0ds.

The Reynolds Club is an organisation of past Students of the Royal Academy Schools. Chairman, Miss Constance-Anne Parker, 1 Melrose Road, Barnes, London sw13, Hon. Secretary: Miss Faith Sheppard and Miss Gwen Webb, Hon. Treasurer: Miss Pauline Sitwell.

The Royal Academy Trust

Chairman

The Lord Lever of Manchester

Managing Trustees

H.R.H. The Prince Philip, Duke of Edinburgh, K.G., K.T.

The Lord Butler of Saffron Walden, K.G., C.H.

Sir Hugh Casson, K.C.V.O., P.R.A.

Roger de Grey, Esq., R.A.

Nicholas Goodison, Esq.

Frederick Gore, Esq., R.A.

John Hayward, Esq.

Air Commodore the Hon. Sir Peter Vanneck, G.B.E., C.B., A.F.C., A.E., M.E.P.

Trustee

Dr. Armand Hammer

The Royal Academy has formed a Trust to which donations and bequests may be made to help ensure the continuity of the activities of the Royal Academy.

The Chairman and Trustees wish to record their gratitude to those who have so generously supported the Trust in its early stages:

Dr. Armand Hammer £170,000

The Manifold Trust £100,000

Friends of the Royal Academy

Patron: H.R.H. The Duke of Edinburgh, K.G., K.T.

Friends:

£15.50 annually.

Friends (Concessionary):

£12.50 annually for Museum Staff and Teachers, £10.00 annually for Pensioners and Young Friends aged 16–25 years. Gain free and immediate admission to all Royal Academy Exhibitions *with a guest* or husband/wife and children under 16. Obtain catalogues at reduced price. Enjoy the privacy of the Friends' Room in Burlington House. Receive Private View invitations to various exhibitions including the Summer Exhibition. Have access to the Library and Archives. Benefit from other special arrangements, including lectures, concerts and tours.

Artist Subscribers:

£22.50 annually.

Receive all privileges shown above. Receive free submission forms for the Summer Exhibition. Obtain art materials at a reduced price. Obtain constructive help where the experience of the Royal Academy could be of assistance.

Sponsors:

£500 (corporate)

£100 (individual) annually.

Receive all the privileges offered to Friends. Enjoy the particular privileges of reserving the Royal Academy's Private Rooms when appropriate and similarly of arranging evening viewings of certain exhibitions. Receive acknowledgement through the inclusion of the Sponsor's name on official documents.

Benefactors:

£1,000 or more.

An involvement with the Royal Academy which will be honoured in every way.

Benefactors and Sponsors

BENEFACTORS

Mrs. Hilda Benham
Lady Brinton
Mr. & Mrs. Nigel Broackes
The John S. Cohen Foundation
The Colby Trust
The Lady Gibson
Jack Goldhill, Esq.
Mrs. Mary Graves
D. J. Hoare, Esq.
Sir Antony Hornby
Irene and Hyman Kreitman
The Landmark Trust
Ronald Lay, Esq.
The Trustees of the Leach Fourteenth
  Trust
Hugh Leggatt, Esq.
Sir Jack Lyons, C.B.E.
The Manor Charitable Trustees
Lieutenant-Colonel L. S. Michael,
  O.B.E.
Jan Mitchell, Esq.
The Lord Moyne
Mrs. Sylvia Mulcahy
G. R. Nicholas, Esq.
Lieutenant-Colonel Vincent Paravicini
Mrs. Vincent Paravicini
Richard Park, Esq.
Phillips Fine Art Auctioneers
Mrs. Denise Rapp
Mrs. Adrianne Reed
Mrs. Basil Samuel
Eric Sharp, Esq., C.B.E.
The Revd. Prebendary E. F. Shotter
Keith Showering, Esq.
Dr. Francis Singer
Lady Daphne Straight
Mrs. Pamela Synge
Harry Teacher, Esq.
Henry Vyner Charitable Trust
Charles Wollaston, Esq.

CORPORATE SPONSORS

Barclays Bank International Limited
Bourne Leisure Group Limited
The British Petroleum Company
  Limited
Christie Manson and Woods Limited
Christie's South Kensington Limited
Citibank
Consolidated Safeguards Limited
Courage Limited
Debenhams Limited
Detta Group p.l.c.
Ford of Europe Incorporated
The Worshipful Company of
  Goldsmiths
The Granada Group
Arthur Guinness Son and Company
  Limited
Guinness Peat Group
House of Fraser Limited
Alexander Howden Underwriting
  Limited
IBM United Kingdom Limited
Imperial Chemical Industries Limited
Lex Service Group Limited
Marks and Spencer Limited
Mars Limited
The Worshipful Company of Mercers
Midland Bank Limited
The Nestlé Charitable Trust
Ocean Transport and Trading Limited
  (P.H. Holt Trust)
Ove Arup Partnership
Philips Electronic and Associated
  Industries Limited
Playboy Club International
The Rio Tinto-Zinc Corporation
  Limited
Rowe and Pitman
The Royal Bank of Scotland Limited
J. Henry Schroder Wagg and Company
  Limited
Seascope Limited
Shell UK Limited
Thames Television Limited
J. Walter Thompson Company Limited
Ultramar Company Limited
United Biscuits (U.K.) Limited
Waddington Galleries' Limited
Watney Mann and Truman Brewers
  Limited

INDIVIDUAL SPONSORS

The A.B. Charitable Trust
Mrs. John W. Anderson II
Mrs. Ann Appelbe
Dwight W. Arundale, Esq.
The Rt. Hon. Lord Astor of Hever
The Rt. Hon. Lady Astor of Hever
Miss Margaret Louise Band
A. Chester Beatty, Esq.
Godfrey Bonsack, Esq.
Peter Bowring, Esq.
Mrs. Susan Bradman
Cornelis Broere, Esq.
Jeremy Brown, Esq.
Derek Carver, Esq.
Simon Cawkwell, Esq.
W. J. Chapman, Esq.
Alec Clifton-Taylor, Esq.
Henry M. Cohen, Esq.
Mrs. Elizabeth Corob
Mrs. Yvonne Datnow
Raphael Djanogly, Esq., J.P.
Mrs. Gilbert Edgar
Brian E. Eldridge, Esq.
Mrs. Erica C. Eske
Friedrich W. Eske, Esq.
Mrs. Myrtle Franklin
Victor Gauntlett, Esq.
Lady Gibberd
Peter George Goulandris, Esq.
Mrs. Penelope Heseltine
J. Home Dickson, Esq.
Geoffrey J. E. Howard, Esq.
Mrs. Patricia D. Howard
Mrs. Manya Igel
J. P. Jacobs, Esq.
Mrs. Christopher James
Alan Jeavons, Esq.
S. D. Kahan, Esq.
David J. Kingston, Esq.
Beverly Le Blanc
Graham Leggatt-Chidgey, Esq.
H. V. Litchfield, Esq.
Owen Luder, Esq.
A. Lyall Lush, Esq.
Mrs. Graham Lyons
Jeremy Maas, Esq.
Ciarán MacGonigal, Esq.
José Martin, Esq.
Peter Ian McMean, Esq.
Princess Helena Moutafian, M.B.E.
David A. Newton, Esq.
P. D. Northall-Laurie, Esq.
S. H. Picker, Esq.
John Poland, Esq.
Dr. L. Polonsky
Dr. Malcolm Quantrill
Cyril Ray, Esq.
Mrs. Margaret Reeves
The Rt. Hon. Lord Rootes
The Hon. Sir Steven Runciman
Sir Robert Sainsbury
Mrs. Pamela Sheridan
R. J. Simia, Esq.
Steven H. Smith, Esq.
Thomas Stainton, Esq.
Cyril Stein, Esq.
Mrs. A. Susman
Mrs. G. M. Susman
K. A. C. Thorogood, Esq.
Sidney S. Wayne, Esq.
Frank S. Wenstrom, Esq.
Humphrey Whitbread, Esq.
David Whitehead, Esq.

There are also 4 anonymous sponsors